PRAISE FOR *SWIM*

"The insights found within the.. ₚₐ... compelling. Barry's refreshing vulnerability regarding his own preconceptions profoundly provoke us to consider our own. He challenges us to think more deeply, behave more compassionately, and evaluate our choices more carefully as we walk out this kingdom journey. The entries are brief, engaging, and reflect a rich trove of well-earned wisdom."

— Janice Wood, Ph.D. Executive Pastor, Vineyard Community Church Richmond (Richmond, Kentucky) author of *Tag: the Art of Discipling*

"Deeply personal reflections that lead us to a deeply personal God. Barry's introspection is both inspiring and convicting moving me closer to God and longing for those I lead to walk with a bolder faith. Barry is both a gentle and strong guide for our restless times. I'm grateful for this simultaneous kick in the pants and arm around the shoulder."

— Darin Mirante, MAC. Lead pastor at First Church of Christ (Burlington, Kentucky)

"Barry's use of personal experience in teaching practical lessons about struggle, faith, and hope resonates with me profoundly. 'Swimming' is a thought-provoking devotional that challenges us and reminds us to be mindful of God's existence in everything."

— Christopher Mueller, MSSW, Alcohol and Drug Counseling Specialization, University of Louisville-Kent School of Social Work, Owner-SofaBurn Records (Dayton, KY)

"If you're tired of a surface-level relationship with God, *Swimming in the Ocean* will guide you to deeper spiritual waters. I felt, at turns, challenged, encouraged, convicted, and inspired by the readings and reflection questions. Whether you're searching for a transformative personal devotional or a meaningful small group discussion guide, you'll find it in *Swimming in the Ocean*."

— Christine Luken, Financial Lifeguard and Author of Money is Emotional: Prevent Your Heart from Hijacking Your Wallet

"Through stories invoking laughter and tears, joy and heartbreak, Barry invites the reader out into the deep waters of soul work. This 52-week devotional study contains a lifetime of stories and learning as Barry illustrates how we're called to not stay in our safe, chlorinated pools, but rather to swim in the wild and dangerous ocean waters that mark life in Christ. Barry is an excellent swim instructor whose writing illustrates that soul work is indeed the work of a lifetime – and it is work that we all must do."

— Thomas Lyons, Instructor and Ph.D. Candidate, Asbury Theological Seminary

SWIMMING IN THE OCEAN

52 Devotions on Plunging into God's Abundant Life

SWIMMING
IN THE
OCEAN

52 Devotions on Plunging into God's
Abundant Life

BARRY M. LONG

For France,

My friend, partner, and number one fan.

TABLE OF CONTENTS

Note: A topical reading guide can be found at the end of this book, beginning on page 207.

FOREWORD

To spend a day with Barry Long is akin to an invigorating walk with no particular agenda. Even without working from a plan, I can predict the outcome of that day — massive deposits of encouragement.

Barry is a lot like a mobile intravenous bag of Vitamin "E" — encouragement. That version of Vitamin E is the most important of all. With it, we prosper. Without it, we can't even function.

As I got over a lengthy hospitalization, he insisted that taking me to a Bob Dylan concert would aid in my recovery. Till our last day neither of us will forget all the sights and smells of a bona fide Dylan concert. As much as anything, just hanging out with a guy who gives away encouragement makes any day a worthwhile investment. The net net of the evening was I came away tired, but my encouragement tank was full.

The next best thing to spending a day with Barry is to read this book. I found this to be, like Barry himself, a deposit of courage. At the close of our high school years, some friends and I took a trip to Lake Powell in northern Arizona. It is a remarkable place to visit as long as you return intact. I made it through a near drowning and made a decision that I will steer clear of swimming in dark water. I'm fine watching people swim in a place like the ocean — just don't ask me along on that journey.

Barry loves to swim in settings; some reasonable people would consider dangerous. When it comes to the ocean, my goal has been to watch and listen to the sounds but steer clear of all water. Barry likes to venture into the ocean to swim with all sorts of interesting and scary creatures, even when he doesn't know how deep the deep of the actual ocean goes any more than the depths of knowing God. Yet he swims in both and invites us to join him.

I'm not sure I'm any closer to swimming in literal dark waters than when I was in high school, yet as I read this book, I feel called to the greater spiritual depth where Barry invites us to swim.

The rewards are worth all the risk and investment of time and effort. Let's spend the next chapter of our lives dedicated to flowing with the very courage and encouragement of God. After all, we were made for swimming in the depths of God.

> — Steve Sjogren, Pastor emeritus of Vineyard Community Church in Cincinnati. They are listed as one of the most influential churches of the 20th Century (*The Ten Most Influential Churches of the 20th Century*, Dr. Elmer Towns)
>
> SteveSjogren.com
> KindnessOutreach.com

INTRODUCTION

Dear Friends,
If we have a choice, the environment we choose to immerse ourselves in can change everything. Jesus calls us to pick him and his full life (John 10:10b), and as his story documents, such a life is not 'easy street.' It is marked by purpose, pain, and joy beyond our wildest dreams if we are willing to risk the plunge.

In the first reading, I report an experience that ended up as a metaphor for the risky, wonderful business of following Jesus, I call it "Swimming in the Ocean." The metaphor can also be applied to anything in life that is positive and worth doing. But, my guiding interest in producing this book is inspiring Christ followers, or those thinking about doing so, with meditations and challenges on how to be skilled swimmers. They invite us to get better; alert us about where sharks lurk and warn us about the dangers of swimming solo.

I hope the readings engender thoughtful conversations among friends or small bible study groups that result in somehow making their pursuit of God more fruitful and passionate. The first reading defines the environment the writer (me) wants to choose but sometimes does not. I bet I'm not the only one who struggles with these choices; in fact, the notion that there are armies of others out there who struggle, too, inspired this project.

Collected within this book are fifty-two weekly readings to guide you through one year of ocean swimming. The Biblical quotes in each reading are from the New International Version unless otherwise cited. The reflective questions at the end of each reading are invitations to go deeper on your own or with friends in a small group setting. Do not allow the questions to limit your reflections on the reading. They are merely conversation starters.

My hope in this project is to inspire a quiet enthusiasm in the reader. The word enthusiasm is rooted in the Greek word "entheos" meaning, possessed by God, or inspired. While the word was used as a pejorative in the ancient world to describe overzealous believers, I pray it might take on a more literal sense for those who use this material. May you be filled with God.

Blessings,
Barry

SWIMMING IN THE OCEAN

M y love of beaches and the oceans goes back to my childhood. Not so much being in the ocean, as watching it, being near it. I prefer swimming in human-made concrete pools with bright, clean, chlorinated water.

Back in 1970, my father purchased a condo in a new high-rise on the Atlantic Ocean. There's a magnificent pool on the southeast deck a mere 30 feet above beach level. I begin each visit with a walk to the pool deck, take in the living seascape, and whisper a prayer of thanks.

Most of the longtime residents at Plaza South believe they've found paradise. And maybe they have because God has often met me in that place, and spoken to me, but never more clearly than he did a few summers ago.

Ezekiel, one of the residents of Paradise, and a great vacation friend inspired these readings. His family calls him "Hess" for short. He is an Iraqi Jew, not "Orthodox" but very serious about his faith. We've had many conversations about Jews, Jesus, and spirituality.

Hess is a lovable joker, loud and boisterous but, somehow not obnoxious. His English makes me laugh, but I bet my attempts at Arabic are just as hilarious to him. I mention this because sometimes it's hard to tell when my friend is serious.

One afternoon, he approached me just after I'd completed my daily laps in the swimming pool. I was sitting in a lounge chair, staring at the ocean, in that relaxed, dreamy state one feels after vigorous exercise.

"Barry," he said at his usual high volume, "why do you always swim in the pool but never the ocean?"

I thought, Ok, this is Hess messing with me, again. So, I shot back, "Because I have a brain, Hess. Think it through. Swimming in the pool is easier, and I don't have to deal with sand in my shorts, salt in my eyes or waves knocking me around; not to mention the part about shark bait!"

He just stood there, shaking his head slowly with a perplexed look on his usually happy face, so I went on the offensive.

"Ok, big boy. Tell me, why you always swim in the ocean instead of the pool?" (Hess only swam in the pool when the Atlantic was too rough.) Now, his facial expression was quizzical as if the answer to my question should have been obvious. "Why?" he began, his voice slowly rising with intensity, "LIFE," he blurted. "There's life in the ocean." He turned and walked away without another word.

Sometimes revelation is like igniting a high-powered flashbulb in a dark room, large quantities of information imprint your brain instantly.

Most Christians, including me, have not developed proper antenna to hear someone outside the church speak prophetically to them. But on that day God punched me in the solar plexus. Hess, true to his namesake Ezekiel, had expressed the word of the Lord to me and I knew it even if he didn't. I got up from the lounge chair and staggered away to a less public place where I could think and pray.

The message was deceptively simple: I was awakened to the fact that I had been swimming in a chlorinated pool—lifeless, sterile and confining. But, life with God was like swimming in the open sea; in a sense, God was the ocean.

Suddenly, things were crystal clear; the ocean even tasted alive; it was full of life. On the other hand, pool swimming was an easy thing to fall into. After all, one is swimming, pool water is wet, and the effort is tiring, so tiring it often leads to boredom and burnout. It's a grind, a routine I'd forced myself into; all signs that life was missing.

Upon reflection ,there were several reasons I was swimming in the pool, not least of which was, I was the pastor of a growing church. I had begun to think of our growth as something to protect. Thus, risk-taking was happening less often among us. Listening for the voice of the Spirit was giving way to a "best practice" mentality. Of course, sound organizational practice is great but listening to God is irreplaceable.

I'd also gotten the idea that I'd done my tour at sea and arrived at the port. We were a thriving church, and I was a decent pastor by most current methods of keeping score. It was "Miller time." I could afford to float in the pool awhile.

Finally, like most Christ-followers I know, it had become easier to avoid the change, pain, and uncertainty that go with ocean swimming. And this didn't only apply to my job as a pastor but to following Jesus daily. I'd slipped into the safe, predictable, controllable pool, where there were no sharks, barracuda, jellyfish, riptides, hurricanes, risks… or life.

The dirty little secret of pool swimming is this: it's not safe at all. The sterile environment of a chlorinated pool kills. (Try pickling your aquarium fish in a chlorinated pool for a few hours.) Pool swimming was deceitfully toxic.

My experience at Plaza South felt like a brand new revelation to me, but it was more like lightning through a lost idea. I'd been in the pool often during my sojourn, and like a good lifeguard, Jesus had pulled me out of danger. He got my attention with circumstances, the creation, people like Hess, and even preachers.

Charles Du Bos wrote, "The most important thing is this: to be ready at any moment to sacrifice all we are for what we can become."[1]

Pool swimmers are unwilling to do this, but what Du Bos wrote is very closely aligned to what Jesus commanded his followers to do (Luke 14: 26,27; 33).

Following this difficult calling promises plumbing new depths in God and surprising new vistas of self-discovery. In fairness, it is dangerous too, but different than being pickled in the pool.

As I swim with God, sharks may well attack, undertows and tsunamis may terrify—all regular ocean swimmers can count on such difficulties (John 15:18-21; 2 Timothy 3:12,13). As Thomas Merton observed: "There is no spiritual life without persistent struggle and conflict."[2]

But, if I'm awake and clinging to Jesus in crisis or storms, God teaches me to become more like the Master. Such things do not happen in the pool. There is more life with one dip in the ocean than a thousand years in chlorine.

After all, Jesus told us: "I have come that they may have life and life to the full" (John 10:10b).

Ocean swimming is the "full" life Jesus promised if we are willing to take the plunge.

The 'life' Jesus speaks of is full but not safe. Authentically following Jesus IS Ocean Swimming. Hess was and is right.

QUESTIONS FOR REFLECTION AND DISCUSSION:

1. Who is the most magnificent ocean swimmer you know? What do you admire about them?

2. How would you describe your usual place of swimming, pool or ocean?

3. In what area of your life is God challenging to get out of the pool and swim in the ocean? How will you do it?

4. What other thoughts or questions does this reading stir in you?

END NOTES:

1 Du Bos, Charles. *Approximations. Quartrieme Serie I.* Paris: Correa 1922.

2 Merton, Thomas. *Life and Holiness.* New York: Doubleday Press, 1963.

CHURCH MEETINGS

I grew up in the Methodist church catching, as the old saying goes, just enough of the good news to inoculate me to the real thing.

I'm not blaming the church, but for me in those days, church meetings seemed like a religious vacuum not connected at all with God, or my other activities—unless I felt guilty about those activities because of something I'd heard in church.

After my conversion, I began to understand I could never do without the gathering of the saints. I would spend the rest of my life honing the ocean swimming skills I learned in church.

Church meetings, properly understood, are dangerous. Paul says, "In church, the secrets of people's hearts are sometimes revealed, and they know God is Present" (1 Corinthians 14:25). The book of Acts reports a prayer meeting where the room was shaken, as in an earthquake (Acts 4:31).

When God is present among believers, all bets are off—anything can happen when the church gathers. Meeting with God in the church is awesome and not a little scary. Annie Dillard's warning about corporate worship makes sense to me.

"Why do people in church seem like cheerful, brainless tourists on a packaged tour of the Absolute? ... Does anyone have the foggiest idea what sort of power we blithely invoke? Or, as I suspect, does no one believe a word of it? The churches are children playing on the floor with their chemistry sets, mixing up a batch of TNT to kill a Sunday morning. It is madness to wear ladies' straw hats and velvet hats to church; we should all be wearing crash helmets. Ushers should issue life preservers and signal flares; they should lash us to our pews. For the sleeping god may wake someday and take offense, or the waking god may draw us to where we can never return."[1]

I've been in church meetings something like that—where one can barely rise from one's seat for the weight of God's glory. Where God drastically changes the course of people's lives, sometimes sending them to far-off places to share his kingdom with folks they've never met. Or when in church services besetting sins are called out by the Spirit in the hearts of worshipers resulting in repentance, forgiveness and new beginnings.

Anything can happen in church. I once saw—right in the front row—a mass deliverance in the middle of a sermon I was preaching in Mozambique, Africa. (For me, it was shocking and disorderly, but not for God.) All I knew to do was keep preaching as others ministered to the liberated. The church can be dangerous, in a lovely way.

Need I mention that most church meetings are not always as dramatic, as the examples above. So, for busy preoccupied folk like us, church can even seem dull and repetitive. We become like Dillard's "cheerful, brainless tourists on a packaged tour of the Absolute."

But the truth is, whenever the church gathers, God is present, and things are happening. Trust me.

Sometimes we see these things with our eyes, often not, which makes perfect sense if one buys into two things: God is present, and the world is both seen and unseen.

QUESTIONS FOR REFLECTION AND DISCUSSION:

1. When your church meets are you like Dillard's "cheerful, brainless tourist?" or expecting to encounter the "Absolute"?

2. Describe an encounter with the "Absolute" you experienced in church. Has it made you a better ocean swimmer? How?

3. What would change about how you prepared for worship if you believed God was present?

4. What other thoughts or questions did the reading stir in you?

END NOTES:

1. Dillard, Annie. Teaching a Stone to Talk: Expeditions and Encounters. New York: Harper & Row, 1982.

A FUNERAL

Some years ago, I attended the funeral of a friend's aunt in a small, country church. The building was right out of the mid-twentieth century, clapboard exterior, and a classic steeple in the front; no fancy stuff.

I walked into the little building with a few others from our church and noted a man across the room afflicted with some debilitating, muscular issue. His twisted body seemed to be pulling in different directions when he moved; it looked painful. When he spoke, it was halting, strained and broken.

I'm ashamed to say that part of me wants to run *away* from visible brokenness in others. Shouldn't Christ followers run *to* the broken? One way I distance myself from such uncomfortable feelings is by defaulting to theological reflection.

"A funeral, I thought; a scene of death, the ultimate enemy. A physically challenged man, another product of 'the fall' which God never intended. Yes, this is indeed a profound picture of our broken, half-baked world." Then, without warning, my abstract, theological meditation took a shocking, revelatory turn. The afflicted man began to struggle toward the platform. He was the dead woman's preacher, and the pastor officiating the funeral service.

In his frumpy, ill-fitting suit, he spoke in herky-jerky fits and starts that would have been comic were they not so tragic. Being in the preaching business myself, I wondered how he would pull it off. I was embarrassed for him and began to squirm a bit in my seat. But a minute into his message I was riveted. His sermon was compelling.

As I meditated on this unexpected, revelatory slice of life, I no longer felt sorry for the preacher's physical limitations. Instead, I saw myself turned inside out.

The struggling speaker and I were alike. The effects of the fall were publicly on display in his body, but I wore mine where no one could see them. We were both broken men preaching the good news of the resurrection, out of the jaws of death.

That day, I learned a little more about humility, ignorant pre-judgments and, most importantly, undying hope. In short, I was a little better ocean swimmer; God was etching me into a disciple of Jesus.

QUESTIONS FOR REFLECTION AND DISCUSSION:

1. I "distanced" myself from the physically afflicted preacher via theological reflection. Do you distance yourself from the brokenness you see in the world? How do you do it? Why?

2. How has your perception of outer brokenness in others conditioned your thinking about them?

3. Think of a relationship where the visible brokenness of the other obscures your own. What is Jesus calling you to do (Matthew 7:1-5)?

4. What other thoughts or questions did the reading stir in you?

A JOURNEY BENEATH
THE SKIN

One morning, I was sitting on the shore of the Atlantic staring at a beautiful seascape and worshipping quietly; I closed my eyes to pray a bit. Another seascape appeared, no doubt imprinted on my mind's eye by the first one.

But my inner ocean was different, dark, moody, roiling and dangerous. It registered deeply that this inner space was (as many ocean swimmers have attested) much more massive than I ever imagined.

I was afraid, as it was largely uncharted territory for me. What if I ran into monsters or got lost and couldn't find my way back? I was not inclined to begin such a mapping project.

I did, however, believe Jesus was Lord of all oceans, no matter how chilling, dark or raging and that he promised never to leave me. I now realize the inner frontier graphically portrayed to me that morning is territory I've been trying to map for 40 years.

I once heard a renowned scholar talk about the inner conflict between human selfishness and obedience to God as an example of the conflict between Satan's kingdom of darkness and God's kingdom of light. He cited the coming of Jesus as the invasion of heaven into our rebellious world to restore the rule of the rightful king. But the kingdom of God doesn't only come "out there" as in God bringing justice or help to the poor or heal the sick. God's kingdom also comes within. God wants dominion in my private world. Until Christ returns to wrap things up, there will be a fight. Paul mentions this inner conflict in his letter to the Galatian church.

> "For the sinful nature (flesh) desires what is contrary to the Spirit, and the Spirit what is contrary to the sinful nature. They are in conflict with each other so that you do not do what you want." (Galatians 5:17)

Dr. John Walton in his book, *The Lost World of Genesis,*[1] personalizes the space outside of God's kingdom as inhabited by "chaos creatures." I call them "ego creatures." They are demonic forces of havoc and disorder that threaten God's good creation. We could give them names like Greed, Fear, Lust, Gluttony, Shame, and other descriptors of what the Bible calls sin.

In my inner world, just as in the "world out there," God's kingdom is present but not fully come. When God's rule comes—light comes, chaos creatures scatter like cockroaches when the light is switched on in a darkened kitchen. When the kingdom comes, disorder resolves into harmony with God's purpose.

Sometimes, I'm so fearful of the "chaos creatures," I don't want to face them. I'd rather deny they exist and leave them in the darkness.

I've employed Christian counselors to help me shine God's light into my inner world and highly recommend the practice. The classic spiritual disciplines also become invitations to God to illuminate and tame my inner space.

The Bible indicates we can enjoy remarkable victory over the deadly, egomaniacal chaos creatures that haunt our inner worlds. The indwelling Spirit of light causes the cockroaches to scramble away and enables me to change my behavior and thinking (Romans 12:1-4). Allowing God to rule in my inner world is key to being a successful ocean swimmer not least because it releases remarkable inner peace. When God reigns inside, I become a more useful instrument in the world "out there."

QUESTIONS FOR REFLECTION AND DISCUSSION:

1. How far along are you in mapping your inner space?

    a. Not, far. It's too frightening.

    b. With God's leadership, I'm beginning the process.

    c. I'm stuck.

2. Can you name your "chaos creatures"?

3. How might Jesus lead you in a "journey beneath the skin"? How can the church help?

4. What other thoughts or questions did the reading stir in you?

END NOTES:

1. Walton, John H. *The Lost World of Genesis One*. IVP Academic. 2009

HEROES

Twenty years ago—my friend, Tom, rescued a lady who lost control of her car and ran it into a lake located in the middle of our subdivision. My friend Tom is a hero.

As a child, Tom was a victim of the 1950s polio epidemic robbing him of the use of his right leg. But that did not stop him from promptly diving into the lake to rescue the desperate lady. (Later, he did again for a small child; they have since put barriers around the lake.)

Tom is brave, but he also knew what he was doing. In spite of his physical challenges, he was a powerful swimmer. He mastered many different strokes and swimming skills over the years including the 'Shepard's Crook' technique, used to haul swimmers in distress out of the water to the shore.

Tom's story can be used to represent how the skills we learn in church prepare us to swim in the ocean. The years of discipline and practice enabled Tom to save the lady who was sinking, fast. In the same way honing the skills of prayer, service, giving, fasting, meditation, and other disciplines can prepare us to show others the rescue found in Jesus. Or not.

Had Tom not developed his swimming skills, his capacity to help the woman would have been absent. And when Christ followers do not develop spiritual disciplines, our ability to join Jesus in rescuing others wanes.

Christians through whom Jesus moves in power are familiar with Jesus, because they have spent time engaged with him, serving with him, listening to him, learning about his concerns. They practice their skills daily, alone and together and in the process are being shaped into heroes, like Tom.

They would never call themselves heroes, most of them, like Tom will never make the evening news, but they are changing the world.

Don't think you have much to offer, walk with a limp? God specializes in expressing his strength through our weakness—if we show up for practice. We show up, God does the healing, strengthening and equipping. The pay-off is discovering the meaning of life, which is giving our lives away in love for the benefit of others.

When the church is working, it works just like that. God's new community takes challenged people like me and helps us toward wholeness so we can do the same for others. That's the church Jesus wants, and I think he will get his way.

QUESTIONS FOR REFLECTION AND DISCUSSION:

1. Think about some heroes you know. What makes them heroic?

2. Does your church train heroes? How? Are you a hero in training? What is your training regimen?

3. Where are people drowning in your sphere of influence? What is Jesus calling you to do?

4. What other thoughts or questions does this reading stir in you?

LAUGHING GOD

D allas Willard and other spiritual masters tout silence as the foundation of spiritual formation. I'm an extrovert, so this is challenging for me to say the least. Besides, I live in 21st century North America with unrelenting noise 24/7. I've attempted to spend time in solitude and silence over the years with varied success.

Carl Gutav Jung is credited with saying, "Hurry is not OF the Devil, hurry IS the Devil." Busyness, or hurry, is akin to noisiness, so those who want to be better swimmers must find serene, unhurried spaces. A few years ago, I found the Abbey of Gethsemani, a Cistercian Monastery in Central Kentucky.

Trappist (Cistercian) monks there rarely talk. Little placards on the cafeteria tables say, "Silence spoken here." I learned a lot about being quiet, but more importantly that God has a great sense of humor.

After dinner on my first day at Gethsemani, a brown skinned man dressed in sleeveless sweatshirt and ratty sweatpants approached me at the end of the hallway in the dormitory. He smiled, then looked around in a conspiratorial way, and whispered in a Hispanic accent, "Ola, you a pastor?"

I was confused, the sign read, "Silence spoken here" but to be polite, I whispered, "yes." "Oh," my new friend said, "me too. I'm from Brazil, you?" I brushed him off as politely as I could and moved away quickly. Did the Brazilian not know the rules?

Apparently not because when I saw him again the next day in the cafeteria line, he whispered my ear off so to speak. This time I self-righteously considered reporting the clown. But the folks all around us in the cafeteria seemed not to notice his rebellious outburst. Instead, they continued to heed the dictum, "Silence spoken here." The Brazilian kept whispering to me through the length of the food line. What a jerk. After I had filled my tray, I moved to a seat apart at a table with one chair where he couldn't follow me.

Next morning, I had recovered from the Brazilian's verbal onslaughts and felt peaceful inside again. I decided to witness the antiphonal chanting the monks did in the chapel, one of the only times the silence rule lifts in that place.

Two lines of cubicles face each other in a long high-ceilinged, beautifully ornate, room. Twice daily, robed monks of the Abbey inhabit the cubicles to chant Psalms back and forth. It is solemn and moving.

I arrived early and sat in an open balcony overlooking the impressive room below. Eyes closed, I dialed down and focused on God. After thirty seconds or so, a pipe organ broke the silence. It sounded like Bach. It was perfect and, thinking the service was starting, I continued to focus, eyes closed, on God.

Then, without warning, the music went sour, creating in me a sensation like fingernails screeching across a chalkboard. My eyes flew open, and, behold, in the room below was my chatty, friend, at the keyboard clad in the scruffy sweat outfit.

My jaws went slack as I stared at the stream of monks in hooded robes filing into the room to take their places in the cubicles. The Brazilian found a cubical too, and no one seemed to notice how wildly ridiculous he looked in his cut off sweatshirt. Apparently, no one noticed him at all. I suppressed a giggle. The chanting of the Psalms began.

Later that day he appeared again and true to form, wanted to talk. He said furtively, "You swim?" Annoyed, I said, "Swim? Yes, sure I guess so." "Come, he said in his thick accent, "I know a lake, we swim, it is beautiful!"

This time, I almost ran away. I stumbled back to my little cell in the dormitory, and plopping on the small bed, I insanely wondered if anyone besides me actually saw the enigmatic Brazilian. Then I laughed out loud until tears came to my eyes.

I bet God laughed too. Maybe, God wants us to smile a lot as we attempt to get better at ocean swimming through disciplines like silence. I don't mean to make light of God; I always take God seriously. I, on the other hand, am a funny, conflicted little creature.

There's a good chance God is laughing at you, too. His chuckle is not mocking or derisive. It's like the laughter parents express when their toddlers are awkwardly learning to walk. The laughing is full of love and affection along with an intense desire for the kid to succeed. Real or not, the Brazilian guy made me laugh and reminded me that God is with me and not mad at me when I fail. God is smiling.

QUESTIONS FOR REFLECTION AND DISCUSSION:

1. Is laughing at yourself hard or easy for you? Explain.

2. How do you judge yourself when practicing the disciplines that lead to successful ocean swimming? (Prayer, study, meditation, silence, fasting, et.)

 a. Lazy

 b. Failure

 c. So, so

 d. Other

3. Which descriptor below most fits how you believe God sees your attempts at the classic spiritual disciplines?

 a. Drill Sargent

 b. Loving Parent

 c. Other

4. What other thoughts or questions did the reading stir in you?

"THINGS HAVE CHANGED"

One morning as I read John chapter 20, my mind was flooded with what was for me a new and very personal understanding of the text. It had become fresh bread as they say.

The passage described resurrection morning when Mary went to Jesus' tomb and found it empty. A line in the second verse captured my attention: "Mary said, 'They have taken the Lord out of the tomb and we don't know where they have put him'" (John 20:2c).

I wrote the following in my journal:

"Things have changed."

Like Mary, I'm searching for Jesus in the last place I found him, but he isn't there. I run around with my hair on fire. "Where have you put my Lord, I cry?" But he has risen, moved on, he is dynamic, alive, leaving empty tombs behind, dying and rising again and bidding me to follow.

When I choose to dwell among the tombs, Jesus calls me by name as he did Mary, "Why look for the living among the dead"?

Jesus is always on the move, doing new things, and the Bible set on fire by the Spirit awakened me as I meditated that day. God was knocking me out of a rut. I needed to follow Jesus to the next adventure rather than try to repeat the past.

Within six months, I set into motion a plan that would bring my 28-year pastorate to an end. It was time for new leadership in our church and my next assignment.

Don't misunderstand; the fresh bread from Scripture was not simply my personal interpretation of the text. Mary also needed to see she could not control Jesus, as the passage makes clear. She even tried to stop Jesus from ascending into heaven, desperately holding on to him (John 20:17)! The Spirit simply made a 'new application' to my situation that day.

Mary and I needed to learn that following Jesus is new and fresh and potentially different day by day. We needed to move with him rather than default to where we last experienced him. Things changed. Mary and I could no longer assume Jesus would do things as he had in the past.

QUESTIONS FOR REFLECTION AND DISCUSSION:

1. Can you relate to Mary's frantic statement: "Where have they put my Lord?" Explain.

2. Think of a few significant changes in your understanding of following Christ.

3. Do you hold on to your former experience of Jesus, as Mary did, or quickly let go of the past and follow him?

4. What, "empty tomb" are you confronting today? How will you find the risen Christ?

5. What other thoughts or questions did the reading stir in you?

READING 8

THE BIBLE

For a follower of Jesus, Spiritual formation for ocean swimming must be anchored in the Bible. My take is the Bible is the most amazing document in the world. I'm sure a Muslim would say, "No it's Quran," a Hindu, "The Vedas," and so on. But as a Christ-follower, the story in scripture is more profound and closer to the reality we see in the world than any spiritual book going. Annie Dillard says it well:

"The Bible, this ubiquitous, persistent black chunk of a best seller, is a chink—often the only chink—through which winds (of eternity or infinity) howl. It is a singularity, a black hole into which our rich and multiple world strays and vanishes. We crack open its pages at [our] own peril. Many educated, urbane, and flourishing experts in many aspects of business, culture, and science have felt pulled by this anachronistic, semi-barbaric mass of antique laws and fabulous tales from far away; they entered its queer, straight gates and were lost. Eyes open, heads high, in full possession of their critical minds, they obeyed the high, inaudible whistle, and let the gates close behind them." (Annie Dillard, The Annie Dillard Reader, pp266) [1]

When I first got involved in reading scripture, I was all about apologetics, defending the book and trying to prove everything was true. I devoured pop-books such as Josh McDowell's "Evidence that Demands a Verdict." I debated New Age guys, Jehovah's Witnesses, Mormons and Christian Science folks.

In those days, it was vitally important to be right and I still think a healthy, high and studied view of scripture is crucial, but I've mellowed on the need to be right.

I don't recall ever arguing anyone into my take on the Bible. Currently, I care far more about whether I'm doing what the Bible says. Arguing for the Bible, as God-breathed is a good thing and understanding the 'story' is essential—but doing what it says is more important (Matthew 7:24-27; James 1:22-25).

As I contemplate scripture, God talks with me and shapes me as a better ocean swimmer. In fact, without the Bible, I'm lost at sea.

QUESTIONS FOR REFLECTION AND DISCUSSION:

1. How important is the Bible in how you direct your every day life? Explain.

2. Are you more passionate about proving the Bible is true or doing what it says?

3. On a scale of one to ten, where does Bible reading/study rate in your consumption of media?

4. What other thoughts or questions did the reading stir in you?

END NOTES:

1. Dillard, Annie. *The Annie Dillard Reader.* Harper Perennial. 1st Edition (1995).

BIBLE WARS AND THE LENS OF JESUS

S adly, what God means for good has also been turned around for evil, even things like the Bible. Scripture has often been 'hijacked' by megalomaniacs, who want to rationalize the pathologies they and their followers embrace by using the name of God.

Sadly, true believers who think they know the precise meaning and nuance of every line of scripture and believe they must fight to defend their views have also misused the Bible. The problem is, the sin disease afflicts true believers too, and often we don't play nice. Things of ultimate importance move us to do things that are unbelievable.

C.S. Lewis put it this way: "The higher the stakes, the greater temptation to lose your temper over the game." Reflections on the Psalms p.28[1]

Sometimes the stakes are quite high, as in the issue of the deity of Christ or his substitutionary death. Other times, they are inflated beyond belief as in the Texas Churches of Christ who once split dozens of ways on the crucial question of whether communion bread should be one loaf or distributed in pieces!

After 40 years of observing (and sometimes taking part in) the rancorous divisions over silly things in church, I've come to the following opinion. Jesus must be the lens through which I understand the story of God in the Bible. This observation is by no means original to me, but it does make sense to me. If Jesus is the lens, we are not killing each other or condemning each other. If Jesus is the lens, we are speaking what we understand as the truth in love, not condescension or rancor. If Jesus is the lens, we love even our enemies.

But if Jesus is the lens, the next question is, "which Jesus?" There is the 'Jesus Seminar Jesus,' the wandering cynic philosopher Jesus, the icon Jesus hanging on the wall of the church, the Civil War slaveholder's Jesus, Jesus the Communist, and Jesus the talisman on the dashboard of the car, just to name a few.

All this drives me to the Jesus of the Gospels, which is always a good thing. The Jesus found there refuses to be co-opted. The Jesus of the New Testament refused when the people tried to make him king (John 6:15). This Jesus is beyond manipulation, he is already king, God's king. He does not fit conventional paradigms, in fact, he often contradicts the deepest traditions and values we learn as children.

For example, Jesus' love and the inclusion of all people, even enemies (Matthew 5:44 ff), challenges my deepest fears and biases. I sometimes don't want to obey the New Testament Jesus, but there he is all up in my grill.

On the other hand, Jesus makes absolutist claims about himself, as the only way to God, or that he came, not to bring peace but division (Luke 12:49-53). How can Jesus be so inclusive, on the one hand, but so exclusive and divisive on the other?

Thomas Jefferson's strategy for dealing with parts of the Gospels he couldn't accept was to tear entire pages out! His edition of the New Testament was free of all he considered superstition, etc. As a Deist, Jefferson was uncomfortable with the content as it stood. His artificial Jesus allowed him to have control. Jefferson was not interested in the real Jesus, but one that fit his design, lifestyle, values, and biases.

I have not sliced and diced pages, but I too have often created a Jesus of my liking. But I'm working on allowing the real Jesus to increase and my artificial Jesus to decrease. How does that happen?

It happens when I go back to the Bible. If the Gospels contain inspired records of the real Jesus (and I believe they do), I must approach it humbly. Where I find contradictions or things I don't agree with or understand, I'll remember what one of my mentors, John Wimber, said he once heard from God: "The problem is not up here, John, it's down on your end."

My current strategy is to try to understand the whole "Story of God" through the lens of Jesus. This approach does not cause me to turn off my brain and do less thinking and study, but more! Bible wars might be opportunities for dialogue when approached through the lens of Jesus.

QUESTIONS FOR REFLECTION AND DISCUSSION:

1. What sort of "silly" Bible wars have you seen or experienced? How would it change things to approach the dispute through the "lens of Jesus"?

2. Are there Bible truths for which we must fight? Name a few.

3. How might using the lens of Jesus change your battle plan?

4. How has looking at your life through the lens of Jesus challenged some of your personal beliefs and convictions? How have you responded?

5. What other thoughts or questions did the reading stir in you?

End Notes:

1. Lewis, C.S. Reflections of the Psalms. HarperCollins. New York. 1986

IT ALL COUNTS

I'm thankful for all the help I've had from more experienced swimmers, and if you have not yet found a good mentor, with respect may I suggest you find one pronto. Since soul work is the work of a lifetime, discouragement is always an issue.

One of my mentors is Dave, the closest thing to a Protestant monk I ever met. He reminds me of the old "Star Wars" character, Yoda.

Dave tells me: "Counts, it all does." Ok. Dave doesn't talk like that, but he sure is wise.

"Even when I fail?" I ask. "There is no failure," he tells me. "Whenever you put yourself in the presence of God, you are changed. Sometimes imperceptibly, other times consciously, it all counts."

I think that is part of what Paul is getting at in 2 Corinthians 3:18:

> "Now the Lord is the Spirit, and where the Spirit of the Lord is, there is freedom. And we, who with unveiled faces all reflect the Lord's glory, are being transformed into his likeness with ever-increasing glory, which comes from the Lord, who is the Spirit." (2 Corinthians 3:18 NIV)

Since we are presenting ourselves to God in the disciplines, we are "becoming what we behold," as someone has said. Dave taught me soul work is the work of a lifetime. Did you get that word, work? And I decide by God's grace to do the work, or not.

Don't get me wrong, I'm not suggesting we earn God's favor by praying hard; only the blood of Christ can do that. I'm just saying without allowing God to form me, ocean swimming is out of my reach. I struggle frantically, lost at sea, full of fear and helplessness rather than faith and peace.

QUESTIONS FOR REFLECTION AND DISCUSSION:

1. Rate yourself as a practitioner of spiritual disciplines on a scale of one to five-with five being very disciplined. Explain your answer.

2. Are there spiritual practices that have fallen by the wayside in your busy life because they feel fruitless? What might change if you believed; 'it all counts'?

3. Do you have a mentor? If not, who might that person be?

4. What other thoughts or questions did the reading stir in you?

HEARING GOD

Have you ever eaten one of those fruity Jello salads? You know, the kind with fruit cocktail just below the surface. I love it when my wife makes Jello salad.

One evening, I was watching TV and remembered there was a fruity Jello salad treasure in the fridge. I broke for the kitchen, grabbed bowl and spoon and opened the refrigerator door.

There it was, but there must have been a production snafu—all the fruit pieces in the salad had migrated to one side of the large glass bowl. Without a second thought, I scooped out the fruity part, left the naked Jello part quivering and resumed my seat in the living room to devour my treat.

It was then God spoke to me, "Barry, think about what you are doing." I rarely talk to myself this way, so I'm pretty sure it was God.

Looking at the Jello salad, full of fruit cocktail, I remembered the pathetically unfruited portion left in the fridge for the next person. Yeah, I went back and returned some of my abundant fruit to the naked salad.

Some may want to demystify what I experienced, saying my conscience has been conditioned to bother me when I'm a selfish pig. Maybe. But could it be the conscience is one way God speaks to us, especially in the little day-to-day swimming we do in the ocean? This is not an argument for the Modern romantic idea of listening to your heart and not your head. That sentimentalism is faulty and often destructive. But what if God renews our consciences, and the Holy Spirit nudges us toward doing the right things?

For those who believe, as I once did, that God only speaks in "Biblical proportions" as in the old Cecil B. DeMille film where he communicated to Moses in a deep booming voice while engraving the tablets of the Big Ten with his fiery finger, please reconsider the Jello salad saga above.

If we eliminate the obviously stupid and selfish impressions we receive through a rigorous biblical filter, I think we can be confident that God wants to speak to us all the time. Unless, of course, we demand fiery fingers and booming voices (1 Kings 19:11-13).

QUESTIONS FOR REFLECTION AND DISCUSSION:

1. Think about a time when you believe God spoke to you. How did he do it? How did you know it was God?

2. During your day are you expecting God to speak to you? Why or why not?

3. What would change about day-to-day life if you began actively and aggressively listening for God?

4. What other thoughts or questions did the reading stir in you?

PRAYER AND ACTION

Comedian George Carlin, an atheist, is renowned for criticizing religion and prayer and suggesting that praying is what people do who pretend to care.

More recently, after a terrorist attack in California, news headlines echoed a similar theme. Rich Shapiro wrote in the New York Daily Times, "Prayers aren't working. Your thoughts and prayers should be about steps to take to stop this carnage."[1]

The message is: Prayer is useless; what we need is action.

The judgments are harsh, but I see the point. Prayer, if it's the real thing, must always lead to action. Praying disconnected from doing is not an idea found in the Bible. Prayer and action go together. For example, Jesus commanded his guys to pray and "...ask the Lord of the harvest, therefore to send out workers into his harvest field" (Matthew 9:38b Luke 10:2ff).

Then, he immediately deployed the same guys to go and be workers in the harvest.

"(He,) ...called his twelve disciples to him and gave them authority to drive out evil spirits and to heal every disease and sickness" (Matthew 10:1).

The command to pray and the commission to go was of one piece. If it's possible to be an answer to your prayer, go and do it. Prayer and action complement one another. On the other hand, there is a sense in which prayer is a crucial prelude to action. Otherwise, the action might just be a waste of time.

The New Testament story of Mary and Martha is a good example (Luke 10:38-42). Jesus and his disciples went to visit close friends Martha and Mary near Jerusalem. Apparently, they arrived unexpectedly. Martha was frantic with all the preparations, but Mary sat at Jesus' feet in the position of a learner.

In Jesus' day, women were not included in 'learning' by most Jewish rabbis. Women did what Martha was doing, preparing lunch for the men and Martha—saddled with all the work—was furious! How unfair of Mary! Martha naturally complained to Jesus (you and I would have done the same), but his response is unexpected:

"Mary has chosen the better part."

Really?

One of the threads many have noticed in the story is that Jesus never told Martha to put on an elaborate dinner. She just plowed ahead until he gently rebuked her: "Martha, Martha…you are worried and upset about many things—but few are needed—or indeed only one…" (Luke 10:41-42a TNIV)

Apparently, the 'one thing needed' was what Mary was doing, listening to Jesus.

It follows that we, too, must be dedicated listeners to Jesus before becoming active. Otherwise, how do we know what to do? Thus, prayer (speaking and listening to Jesus) is vitally connected with doing; one without the other is incomplete.

My friend Steve said it well, "Pray before doing the project, pray on the way, pray while doing it, and pray after you do it." Let me share a story that illuminates the wisdom of this approach to Prayer and Action.

I was in a group headed for India in the mid-nineties. We were looking to partner with a church planting movement in the southern part of the nation. The group had already planted a dozen churches, and we were excited about potential involvement.

Before we left, we held several joint prayer meetings, and during one of them, a guy from our team saw a vision, of us, washing the feet of a group of pastors we were to visit. Just before he announced what he believed God had shown him, I also saw a picture in my mind's eye of a human foot caked with mud. So, when my friend shared his picture, I immediately shared mine. Our team concluded that at some point to conduct a foot washing for the pastors we would visit in India.

Not long after our team arrived there, the opportunity presented itself for us to do what we believed we heard in prayer weeks before. We were in a rural area with about 80 Indian pastors, and I was teaching. I had asked the guy who organized the trip to provide pails of water ready for foot washing. Getting the water was no small task with the nearest well about 200 yards downhill from our meeting place. But with some sweat and a few callouses, we made it happen.

I spoke on the subject of servant leadership from John chapter 13, the passage recording Jesus washing his disciples' feet. After the teaching, I announced to the group that we believed the Lord wanted our team to wash their feet. I noted many in the group were mildly shocked.

God knew something we did not know at the time. The pastors harbored a deep-seeded cultural resentment toward white Westerners. They were much too polite to demonstrate this resentment, but it was there. The ill feeling was certainly a hangover from the Colonial period (1858-1947), and the British Raj "We'll teach you to do things properly" attitude many Western missionaries had demonstrated over the years.

The pastors were also divided among themselves due to the old Indian caste system, which, even though outlawed, caused bitterness and resentment between higher castes and so-called lower castes. The ingredients for division and rancor were just slightly below the surface inside the cramped, mud brick building where we gathered. The group was close to outright civil war.

It was no wonder our offer to wash their feet in that atmosphere shocked and disarmed them. Were these Westerners going to humble themselves in this culturally demeaning way? We were, and Jesus used it to place His finger on the strife boiling just below the surface in their hearts. Jesus had their attention.

We knelt to begin washing the feet of the first pastor and heard the sound of soft weeping in the room.

Then, quiet but fervent conversations leaked out between pastors; more soft weeping and then spontaneous embraces. Men were confessing their sins of pride and bitterness to one another. Reconciliation was stirring. God's Spirit fell on the room in loving power.

Our team watched in awe as The Spirit worked. Each new pair of feet we washed was attached to a man in tears, and at length, one of the pastors asked if they could wash our feet. Before long, they were washing one another's feet, weeping, laughing for joy and singing together.

I'd love to take credit for this brilliant ministry idea, but it was Jesus. His Spirit showed up to affect all sorts of healing. The church planting movement there continued and spread.

Individual and corporate prayer are the keys to Christian activism, as Thomas Merton wrote, "Action is the stream and contemplation is the spring."[2] If prayer is not leading to and conditioning the actions I take, I'm much more likely to waste my time or as suggested by Carlin, "Pretend to care." No wonder Jesus said to pray without ceasing.

A persistent prayer life is hard work, and I have often been discouraged in this foundational piece of ocean swimming. In those times, I've had to remind myself that prayer is a marathon, not a sprint. Persistence and showing up is everything.

QUESTIONS FOR REFLECTION AND DISCUSSION:

1. Review George Carlin's suggestion at the top of this reading. In what sense is it "telling"?

2. Have you ever felt the urging of God to take part in the answer to a prayer you were praying? What happened?

3. Are you more like Mary, patiently waiting at the feet of Jesus to see what he wants, or serving your head off like Martha?

4. Is prayer without action like faith without deeds (James 2:14-26)? Why or why not?

5. What action is Jesus calling you to in prayer?

6. What other thoughts or questions did the reading stir in you?

END NOTES:

1. Shapiro, Rich. *God Isn't Fixing This.* The New York Daily Times. December 2, 2015.

2. Merton, Thomas. *No Man Is an Island.* Pg. 73 Shambhala Publications. 2005

NEVER GIVE UP

My father-in-law was one of the nicest men I've ever met, but when it came to the subject of Jesus or Christianity, he was more than skeptical. An attorney by trade, he was a natural debater who loved to ply his son-in-law, the pastor, with typical skeptical questions such as "why does God allow suffering?"

Our conversations were lively and for me, most frustrating. Dad just couldn't believe in things he could not reason his way through, and the story of Jesus—especially the miraculous parts—were just too much for him. My wife and I prayed the better part of 40 years for her parents, and during those years, my mother-in-law became a believer, but Dad was still a holdout at ninety. Our kids and our grandkids joined us in the prayer project.

Our granddaughters, then ages ten and thirteen, committed to praying every day for the 90-year-old lawyer to open his heart to Jesus. But Dad continued to brush aside my gentle, and not so gentle attempts to talk about how Jesus loved him and wanted a relationship with him; that is until his partner of sixty-six years passed.

When longtime lovers part, the one left often begins to decline physically, and Dad did decline. It also frequently happens that when folks undergo trauma or a dramatic dislocation, they begin to reconsider everything. My wife was at Dad's bedside on the last day of his life. She asked if she could pray for him and read to him from the Bible. Oddly he agreed. She was mildly shocked but grateful, and not having a Bible close by, she whipped out her smartphone and clicked onto her daily devotional guide.

The verses she read from the devotional guide seemed strangely to address the very topics Dad needed to hear—repentance, forgiveness, and faith in Christ. Amazingly, after each reading, Dad clearly and firmly said,

"Amen!"

As the old lawyer struggled between life and death, out of the blue, he prayed: "O Lord, please accept me."

I've heard the "sinner's prayer" in many forms, but never one more eloquent than Dad's.

Two of my wife's sisters had also come to their Father's bedside, and a moment after Dad had asked Christ to "accept him," one of them walked into the little bedroom. Neither of the sisters shared our faith in Christ. In fact, in some ways, they are a bit turned off by it. France was overjoyed but confused, asking herself, should I put on a serious, sad face? In the moment, she figured the best strategy was to excuse herself, and she left the room.

Reaching a bathroom down the hall, France entered and began to laugh and cry at the same time. The father she loved and prayed for during the past 40 odd years just exchanged his life for the life of God!

But the wonders were not finished. When France entered the room again, her Dad was singing at the top of his voice: "Jesus loves me this I know for the Bible tells me so." Debbie, one of her sisters, was singing along.

Amused and bewildered my wife said, "Who started the singing?" Rolling her eyes a bit Deb said, "He did!"

By nightfall, Dad was with the Lord.

Jesus knows when we are ready to trust him. My theory is that Dad's skeptical lawyerly mind finally became childlike. I do not mean he was intellectually impaired (he wasn't)— only that the guarded skeptic finally dropped his defenses and became like a child. Prolonged and persistent prayer was also a critical factor. The gift of prayer allows us to participate with God as he saves the world. As someone once said, "We can't do it without God, and he won't do it without us."

Prayer is a marathon, not a sprint, an endurance race for which I need God's grace; ocean currents are strong and the voyage long. For every prayer 'success' story, I have at least ten apparent failure scenarios.

Jesus always asks me the same question when I'm slacking.

"… When the Son of Man comes will he find faith on the earth?" (Luke 18:8b)

In my case, it depends on when he comes. I've dropped some prayers altogether, even some that I was sure Jesus wanted to answer. I'd get hot on a few petitions such as,

"Oh, God destroy the heroin traffic in our community!" or, "Lord, send revival!"

Then stop for months, because I hadn't seen results more quickly and/or my attention span was exhausted. Note to self: Remember your father-in-law.

The pantheon of the heroes of faith listed in Hebrews 11 always challenges me; the writer tells us:

"These were all commended for their faith, yet none of them received what had been promised. God had planned something better for us so that only together with us would they be made perfect." (Hebrews 11:39-40)

QUESTIONS FOR REFLECTION AND DISCUSSION:

1. Share a few remarkable answers to prayer you have experienced.

2. What causes you to give up on your prayers?

3. How do you recognize prayers you should persist in from prayers that you might discard?

4. What are your reflections on the Hebrews 11:39 passage in the reading? How might this text influence the way you pray?

5. What other thoughts or questions did the reading stir in you?

RUNT: PART 1

If someone were to ask, what is it your God does? a
shorthand answer might be, "Our God saves."
Psalm 98 and dozens of other scriptures identify
God as a God who saves (rescues). But what does that
mean?

My Uncle Runt—yep that's what we called him—
full grown, he was pushing 5' 5" but his size belied
who he was. Uncle Runt was not a person to be taken
lightly.

He was a tough little customer who, for thirty years,
supervised a crew of unskilled factory workers
including, ex-cons and crazy troublemakers working
mainly as day laborers. These men worked hard, lived
hard and could be dangerous when provoked. Yet, Runt
commanded their respect. Runt respected them too. But
the part of Runt's story I want to tell happened before
he ran that crew of hardworking misfits. In 1944 during
WWII, he served on a Casablanca-class escort carrier
named, "St. Lo"— formerly christened "Midway."

The ship would become famous as the first
American vessel sunk by a Japanese Kamikaze attack.
She went down at the Battle of Leyte Gulf on October
25, 1944. The suicide bomber penetrated a place on St.
Lo's deck just above a storage area for ammunition and

other explosives. Several heavy explosions followed. They were so violent the ship was torn asunder preventing, many men from deploying to lifeboats. Hundreds of sailors went into the sea; of the 889 on board, 434 survived the ordeal and one of them was Runt.

Runt, whose given name was Adlai, was not technically my Uncle. He was my first cousin's Uncle, but since we lived next door to our cousins, he quickly became my Uncle, too. Runt was one of the friendliest men I ever met, always laughing and cutting up. I never heard him say a mean thing about anyone. Since Adlai already cussed like a sailor, the Navy seemed the right choice, and when the Japanese bombed Pearl Harbor, like many other kids his age, he joined the war effort.

I guess that Runt never thought he'd need rescuing. Teenagers are amazingly naïve when it comes to danger, maybe that's one reason the young are so willing to go to war. The sailors not killed in the attack went into the drink where sharks lurked, and high waves swamped them again and again. Some clung to debris; others piled on the surviving lifeboats. Runt said he heard wounded men in their dying moments cry out for their mothers, others groaning or wailing in panic.

Imagine yourself floating in that ocean of fear. Fear was their constant companion. A fear gnawing at hope like a rat gnaws a lifeline. Death felt nearer than life. Fear of death deals a powerful combination punch to the pit of the stomach; hope seeps away.

"It's a ship!" someone shouted after what seemed like hours.

Then another shout went up. Imagine the thoughts and emotions going through my Uncle's body and mind when he heard those words. Maybe he mistrusted hope;

if it were a false alarm, perhaps the weight of despair would sink him.

But the hope was confirmed, others took up the chorus, and loud cheers rose up among the floating refugees. Now he saw the vessel and joined in, the wide-eyed, adrenalized cheer going up from the floating group of men. A U.S. ship was heading toward them.

Volumes of salty tears of relief must have joined the salty Pacific that day. Massive jolts of pure joy must have pulsed through the men who were lost but now found. I mostly guess about these emotions, as Runt wasn't much for describing emotions. But if this is not a victory- pulled- from- the jaws of defeat- rescue story, I haven't heard one. Followers of Christ celebrate another rescue story. The story is about God becoming one of us to save us from sin, death, and meaninglessness. God's rescue doesn't promise a life without pain or even Kamikaze strikes. (Though I believe Jesus protects us on many occasions.) God promises a life that knows all will be well even when things look horrid.

It knows help is here and will keep arriving, even when your ship's been hit, and the security in which you trusted is blown out from under you, fear cannot sink your heart. For some of us, it is easy to dial up the memory of life on a sea of fear without hope. Such memory is more difficult for those who have never felt apart from Jesus as far as they remember, but our common need for rescue is certain (Romans 3:23).

We who rely on Jesus, whether we are aware of it or not, are pulled out of a raging sea of judgment, but our rescue means far more than skipping hell. We are rescued for the sake of others; our lives are saved for the deep purpose of joining God in saving the world. Runt went back home after the war, led a productive life and reared a healthy, loving family. He brought tons of joy to those who knew him like a man who was just glad to be alive. Runt did not merely live; he lived a life of gratitude, a life that grasped what rescue really means.

QUESTIONS FOR REFLECTION AND DISCUSSION:

1. Recall your conversion. What happened? What difference has it made in your life?

2. How does the reading above help you see the drama of being rescued by Jesus? Explain.

3. If it's true we are rescued for a purpose, how do you understand that purpose in your life today? How are you working it out?

4. When you feel adrift on a sea of fear, what do you do?

5. What other thoughts or questions did the reading stir in you?

RUNT: PART 2
"REAL WORSHIP"

I n the last reading, I shared the story of my "Uncle Runt," who was rescued after his ship was blown asunder by a Kamikaze attack in WWII. I compared it to the rescue Jesus offers those who trust him.

Sadly, unlike my Uncle and his shipmates who were dumped into the Pacific in '44, many religious people and churchgoers do not "get" the need to be rescued. We are somehow blind to our dangerous dilemma (Romans 3:23).

The Pharisees, a strict sect of Judaism, influenced the religious thinking of a significant portion of the Jewish people during the ministry of Jesus. One of them, named Simon, invited Jesus to dinner, not for the purpose of sharing a meal but to subject him to a serious grilling.

Luke 7:34 makes this clear when Jesus points out his host offered him none of the typical basic marks of hospitality such as a welcome kiss and the washing of his feet.

The Pharisees were the "church police" and wanted to find out if this new rabbi was leading the people astray; that is, astray from their power and influence.

Jesus was a free agent not coming to them for approval, which meant he was regarded as a threat.

Enter a desperate woman, who boldly crashes through a formidable cultural barrier, appearing at an all-male event. She was, however, not only driven by desperation; she carried a burning hope that the new rabbi, Jesus, could somehow make things right in her topsy-turvy broken life. Luke doesn't tell us her name, perhaps because what Jesus did for her that evening would wipe out her past and give her a new identity.

She brought a jar of expensive perfume and poured out its sweet-smelling contents upon Jesus' feet, in full view of the scandalized old boys club. The aroma filled the room and ascended to heaven.

Her hair dangerously undone, she wept washing Jesus' feet with her tears using her long hair as a towel to dry them. Seeing her faith, desperation, and sin, Jesus forgave her and drew her out of her personal sea of chaos and fear. To say this was a shocking development would be a massive understatement.

Simon, the host, quickly concluded Jesus could not be a prophet. If he was, he would never allow this wretched whore to touch him much less practically worship him! Didn't he care the woman's touch would make him unclean, according to the purity laws of the synagogue police? Jesus didn't seem to care at all and responded with a story:

> "Two men owed money to a certain money lender. One owed him five hundred denarii (About two years wages) and the other fifty. Neither of them had the money to pay him back, so he canceled the debts of both. Now which of them will love him more?" (Luke 7:41-42)

The answer is obvious, and even Simon got it right, "The one who owed the moneylender more," he said. Jesus then delivered the punch-line of the story: *"You have judged correctly, Simon. Therefore, I tell you, her many sins have been forgiven—for she loved much. But he who has been forgiven little loves little" (Luke 7:47).*

My uncle and the other sailors fished out of the Pacific are, in at least one sense, like the woman who poured costly perfume on Jesus and washed his feet with her tears; they were acutely aware they were shipwrecked and sinking fast. They needed salvation, and when it came, they were giddy, weepy, grateful, and joyous! It might not be a stretch to say their thankfulness was a genuine expression of love for their rescuers like the woman's love for Jesus in our story.

Conversely, Simon and his guys had no clue they too were shipwrecked, drowning, needing rescue. They were the religious gatekeepers, assuming God's acceptance while excluding people like the whore. The gatekeepers were confident in their righteousness, blind to the sin of spiritual pride. The most dangerous sort of transgression is the sort we refuse to see.

Sadly, I can identify with Simon and his cronies, and I'm sure Jesus is calling me to be more like the woman who wept and washed his feet. Perhaps my sins are better hidden than hers. Like Simon, I often hide under religious garb or ignorance. I can tend toward self-righteous judgment of others in half a heartbeat. My antidote is to remember, without my rescuer, I'd still be hopelessly lost at sea or sunk to the bottom.

QUESTIONS FOR REFLECTION AND DISCUSSION:

1. Why do you think Simon, the religious leader, saw himself as different from the woman who anointed

Jesus? Can you identify with Simon's attitude toward the woman? Explain.

2. What might be different in the way you worship if you saw yourself as the woman in Luke's account?

3. Put yourself in the place of the woman in this story. Write a paragraph of worship and thanksgiving to Jesus.

4. What other thoughts or questions did the reading stir in you?

GIVING MONEY

At a conference I attended in Nashville, Tennessee one of the speakers was author Dr. Tony Campolo. He told a story about a meeting he did at a well-heeled Christian women's group near Philadelphia. Below is how I remember his tale.

Dr. Campolo had taken "the red eye" flight from L.A. back to Philly but forgotten about the booking he'd accepted months before with the aforementioned women's group.

Upon his arrival in Philadelphia about 7:00 A.M., he called to check in with his office, and when his assistant reminded him of the 10:00 A.M. engagement, he did not respond well.

He was tired, cranky and not in any mood to do public speaking. He kept his commitment, however, guzzling strong coffee as he drove to the hotel banquet facility where the meeting was to take place.

Upon arrival, Tony was directed to a seat on the dais where a gaggle of impeccably dressed women (presumably, officers of the club.) chatted. Below the dais, the plush room held eighty or so women dressed to the nines, who with Bibles in hand, were looking forward to a morning with Dr. Tony Campolo.

The bejeweled chairwoman of the club, who was to introduce Tony spoke first about a mission project the group had taken on which was $500 short of the commitment the group had made.

(The mission was an orphanage somewhere in the two-thirds world, where, I don't recall from the story.) The host suggested they ask God in prayer to provide for the shortfall to the mission.

At that point, the lady doing the introducing had a spontaneous idea, "Dr. Campolo," she said seeming pleased with herself, "before you speak, why not lead us in prayer for God to provide the balance of our commitment?" Amens were heard from the others in attendance.

"No," Campolo croaked in a low, raspy "early morning hasn't had enough coffee –" voice –"NO!" A collective gasp hissed through the banquet room. "No?" said the lady at the podium.

"I never ask God to provide what I already have," blurted Campolo.

Getting up from his seat on the dais he began with a woman on the end of the first row; "How much cash do you have?" Turning deathly pale, the startled women smiled nervously, looked for help to the chairwoman, who shrugged her shoulders slightly shook her head and lifted her hands palms up in surrender.

The woman Campolo accosted stuttered, "Uh, I think I've got about $75." "Great," said Tony, "that's a start," then moved to the next woman in the front row. "You, how much cash do you have?" And so, it went; they raised the project money before reaching the second row.

This story reminded me of what I heard one old preacher say to his congregation, "We have all the money we need in this church to fulfill our mission;

now I just need to figure out how to get it out of your pockets!"

Did the Campolo story happen in just the way he told it? I don't know, but I have no reason to doubt it. What matters more is the moral of the story, which is nothing short of powerful. We are always asking God to provide what we already have. I know I do.

If you are a North American Christian you may not know it, but you are relatively wealthy, no question. I too am rich. I don't feel guilty about being a North American or being rich—only about not being generous.

Sociologists, Christian Smith, Michael Emmerson and Patricia Snell, wrote a book on American giving called *Passing the Plate: Why American Christians Don't Give Away More Money*. The data in the book is penetrating. They say most Christ-followers don't even come close to the commonly agreed upon standard in the church of ten percent of income.

The fact is Christian giving in North America rolls in just shy of two percent.

For those who believe that tithing is not a New Testament principle, consider tithing as a starting point for giving rather than the endpoint, and you will be closer to a Biblical take on generosity.

Furthermore, Smith and his co-authors assert that if regularly attending church members simply gave ten percent, there would be enough money to take care of our ponderous facility costs, staff salaries, mission budgets, and the poor in our communities. That is shocking.

Generous and sacrificial financial giving indicates the giver has grasped the glorious grace of God while flinty giving reveals a rock-hard heart.

QUESTIONS FOR REFLECTION AND DISCUSSION:

1. Do you consider yourself a generous person? How do you arrive at your assessment?

2. Do you consider yourself a wealthy person? How do you arrive at your assessment?

3. What are the things in our culture that militate against generosity?

4. Where might God be calling you to be more generous?

5. What other thoughts or questions did the reading stir in you?

Reading 17

Authority

Read John 14:12.

I was a member of a mission team led by my friend, Steve, that traveled to Oslo, Norway, in 1988. Our job was to encourage the church there and pray for folks after Steve spoke.

The times of prayer exceeded my expectations, as people were physically healed, empowered, and delivered from demons—sometimes en masse. During a break time, a few team members and I were having tea in the basement of the church.

A contingent of Norwegian men walked in with a guy in tow who looked pale and stressed out. The leader of the little group asked me,

"You people are the Vineyard prayer team from the States, yes?"

Strangely sensing danger, I almost said, "Why do you want to know?" But instead, I owned up.

"Yes, we are."

I turned to find my team, but they had mysteriously disappeared. I was alone sitting on the couch facing the troupe of Norwegians and the pale guy they brought with them.

The spokesman for the group explained that the guy they brought with them had been a famous singer in their country, and recently had become a Christ-follower. The problem was, since his conversion when he would attempt to sing, he gagged, choked and couldn't breathe. Then the spokesman said in what sounded to me like a command,

"You will heal him!"

My feeling of wanting to be somewhere else, anywhere else, grew almost unbearable so, I blurted, "Let's wait for Steve (our team leader) to come back, then we can pray for him, ok?"

"No, you must heal him now." The word "must" sounded like he said it in caps. The demanding tone was, I think a function of his broken English, but that did not dawn on me until later.

Did I mention that sometimes Jesus pushes you into the ocean?

"Sink or swim," he says, and I was going down fast. I frantically searched my brain to remember how our mentor, John Wimber, taught us to pray based on the way Jesus did it in his ministry. Rising from the couch, I kept my eyes open, as I'd been taught and prayed,

"Holy Spirit, I invite you to come and rest on us…"

What happened next shocked me, the man began to choke and seize up. I panicked—how will I explain this to Steve, not to mention the police, why the person I was praying for died?

Instinctively, I looked up for help and spied one of my traitorous team members in the back of the little contingent of Norwegians. She put her index fingers on either side of her head pointing upwards as if they were horns. She was trying to tell me I was dealing with a demon.

No kidding, you deserter I thought, why don't you come and help me! But I was on my own and said rather too loudly, toward the gasping man,

"You evil, unclean spirit, stop it and come out!"

The man violently convulsed, went limp and fell on the couch breathing heavily. Jesus had delivered him. After he calmed down, he sang. He was a good singer, but to me, it was the most beautiful voice I'd ever heard!

The ocean is unpredictable. The Spirit's power is essential. Since that day, I've been used in several deliverances that were "clean" like this one but tons of others that were not so clean. I don't have a deliverance ministry, that's for sure. But I still pray for demonized people, because Jesus is full of love and mercy for those tormented in body and mind. And we are His body, His hands, feet, and voice called to do His ministry in the power of the Spirit.

QUESTIONS FOR REFLECTION AND DISCUSSION:

1. Have you ever felt spiritually inadequate to help a hurting person? How did you respond?

2. I must conclude that God allowed me to experience the situation I told about in my story. Why would God do such a thing?

3. In John 14:12, Jesus said those who believed in him would do greater works than he had done. What do you think Jesus means by this statement?

4. What other thoughts or questions did the reading stir in you?

DRINK IT ALL

Read Matthew 26:26-30; Mark 14:22-24; Luke 22:14-20; John 6; Acts 2:42.

"The Communion table," says scholar N.T. Wright, "is a thin place in the world, a place where the barrier between heaven and earth is skinny."[1] I certainly agree. The Lord's Table is precious and life-giving, a window through which grace can pour nurturing and strengthening as we approach it in faith.

After conversion, I was so full of joy and zeal, I immediately wanted to be involved with serving in some capacity, which was a new thing for me. My usual M.O. in life was to avoid involvement with any group, especially as a volunteer. Those who knew me well would have noticed right away that something had radically changed!

I pestered the pastor most Sunday mornings to let me serve in some way. The first assignment he gave me was setting up chairs in the facility our church rented. When I pressed him for more duty, he promoted me to the team that prepared and served Communion. At that time, the church I went to offered the Lord's Supper once a month. I knew it was a Holy thing, this Communion, but I did not know why, exactly.

A few weeks later, I showed up with another guy on the Communion schedule. I was thrilled and a little nervous. We served the Lord's Supper before the regular service, usually to about fifty people. My fellow server and I passed the elements around to the group before partaking.

We used the Communion wafers the church supply store sold, but unlike the small individual plastic cups we have today, the grape juice was poured into one large chalice to be shared by all. In those days, we were not so freaked out by sipping from a communal cup. That day, the chalice was filled almost to the brim.

After the wafers were handed out, we ate together then passed the cup. Since each communicant took only a small, polite sip, the vessel was still three-quarters full when it came back to my fellow server and me.

Now it was time for us to take Communion. We both swallowed the wafer and the guy serving with me took the aforementioned polite sip from the large cup and passed it along.

Someone or something told me; "Drink it all!" Drink it all? What a strange thought, chugging this juice would look stranger still. No way was I doing that. Again, came the mental prompt, this time with authority, "Drink it all."

I figured, this impression must have come from God, and I was so new in the faith I hadn't learned to talk myself out of obeying his voice, so I threw back my head and chugged the grape juice.

My chugging was a little too energetic, as I gulped grape juice some escaped from both corners of my mouth, streaming down into my ears. My serving partner's weirdo detector went off about then, and he quickly moved away. I felt like a fool.

Another impression came; "Barry, that cup is my love, whenever you get the chance—drink it all, you will need it for where you need to go and what you must do." I got emotional, God's love all over me and down inside me, too.

Later, after some schooling, I began to understand that Jesus' blood is His love poured out for the likes of you and me. His love is required nutrition for those who serve Him. The blood also suggests hard times and suffering. Never politely refuse his love, never worry about looking foolish; always, always drink it all.

QUESTIONS FOR REFLECTION AND DISCUSSION:

1. Does your church take the Lord's Supper regularly? How have you understood the Supper's significance?

2. Have you ever talked yourself out of doing what you thought God might have told you to do? Explain.

3. The violent shedding of Jesus' blood and the love of God seem contradictory to some. How would you describe their relationship?

4. What other thoughts or questions did the reading stir in you?

END NOTES:

1. Wright, N.T. *The Meal Jesus Gave Us*. Westminster John Knox Press, Louisville, KY. 2002 and 2015

RELENTLESS

I n 1989, I led a team on a short-term mission project in Slovakia. We were preaching to people who, for 80 years, were not able to hear the gospel of Christ because of repressive Communism. During one session held at a little movie theater, I spoke about the close association between God's love and the Holy Spirit. I pointed out how the Spirit was, "God, up close and personal," touching not simply our minds by revelation but our emotions with affection and a sense of God's presence.

Paul affirms the juxtaposition of Love and the Holy Spirit in Romans 5:1-8 where he writes about the peace and joy faith in Christ brings.

God sustains us even in our sufferings (Romans 5:3-4). He does this by pouring out his "love in our hearts by the Holy Spirit…" (Romans 5:5) Peace, joy, and comfort are experiences, not academic talking points. I told the group God creates us for a relationship and that relationship includes experience.

At the end of the teaching time, I told them it's possible to 'know the facts' about God's love, peace, and joy but not experience these things. Then I prayed out loud and asked the Spirit to invade us with God's love.

The room was silent for a few moments; then I began to hear people softly weeping, others began to shake visibly, and some wept loudly. People fell to the ground, and it was on. God was opening the inner "soul-scapes" of his people to do healing work.

Our little ministry team had seen this before, and we began to move among them inviting God to pour out more of his love and mercy.

One team member related a story to me later that took my breath away.

She and two others had been praying for a little Finnish woman who spoke almost no English. She came to the team and said, bluntly, through an interpreter, "I never feel God's love." The group gently asked the Spirit be poured out on her in a fresh, revelatory way. There was no response; one team member later described her as a little Finnish rock, hard and closed.

Mary Ann, the team leader, thought she heard the Spirit say, "Sing to her." Understandably uncomfortable with the idea, Mary Ann decided to sing softly using the gift of tongues or what she called her prayer language. So, she gently began the song, oddly, a melody she never heard before; later she said the "tongues" sounded different from her usual 'prayer language.'

During the singing, the 'rock' began to crack, then crumble; the little old woman started weeping, then sobbing.

"God loves me," she cried over and over again in Finnish.

After a short display of pure ecstasy and joy—this mild commotion went on for a few minutes then subsided—Mary Ann asked via our interpreter what had happened; why had the rock crumbled? Get this.

The song Mary Ann sang to the rock was an old Finnish lullaby the woman's grandmother used at bedtime when she was a small child. A lullaby!

Imagine yourself in Mary Ann's place; you have a vague impression about singing to an apparently unreceptive person for whom you'd been praying. Had I been in her shoes, I'd have stayed in the pool where it was safe, prayed a blessing on the little rock and moved on.

Not Mary Ann, no sir, she is an ocean swimmer. She had trained herself in the risky trial and error adventure of listening to God and doing what God says.

Think of it. Had she decided to remain in the chlorinated pool, a lonely soul might have missed the love of God breaking in on that evening. In turn, Mary Ann would not have experienced the life-giving thrill of being God's hands, feet and voice.

QUESTIONS FOR REFLECTION AND DISCUSSION:

1. Explain how God's love found you.

2. How would you describe Mary Ann in our story?

3. What challenges you most about how she served the Finnish woman?

4. Where is God calling you to show relentless love?

5. What other thoughts or questions did the reading stir in you?

WHAT IS A PERSONAL RELATIONSHIP WITH GOD?

Read Romans 5:5; 6:1ff; 8:9,14; 1 Cor. 1:4-9, 6:9-11, 12:13; 2 Cor.1:2ff; Gal. 3:1-5, 4:6f; Col. 2:11ff; 1 Thess. 1:5ff

I never bought into the theology of the Holy Spirit my theology professor at the seminary espoused. No question; he was a brilliant man, but his teaching on the subject of the Spirit seemed more driven by an anti-charismatic bias than Biblical reflection. This conclusion may be an unfair judgment of the motives of a deeply focused Christian with a PhD from a prestigious Ivy League seminary, but that was my take.

He once told our class he was not sure a "personal relationship" with God was a Biblical idea, which got my attention. I began seminary as an older student after following Jesus for about a decade, and my professor's statement contradicted my understanding of the Bible and my life's experience.

We all agree that relating to human beings can include the emotional and the intellectual. We think and feel in our interactions with people. We feel the anger of a miffed friend as well as their love when they are pleased with us. The message I heard in class that day was: Relationship with God, was not personal like the ones we enjoy with other humans.

The professor explained interaction with God as: "We speak to God through prayer, and God communicates to us through the Bible." He also stated that any other messages or experiences we may think we are having with God are dangerous, perhaps even demonic.

I get it, like my Prof., I am a U.S. American with a Western European ancestry where public display of emotion is not encouraged and sometimes even repressed, and—as can be documented—emotions or feelings are often messy or unreliable. In addition, when folks in our culture say things like they hear God speak or feel God's presence, eye rolling is not uncommon as a response.

I should also own the fact that my professor's statement offended and even threatened me a bit considering his high degree of learning. God, however, used it as a stimulus to get me thinking about what I thought I knew and believed.

The infant Ancient Near Eastern church did not eschew emotions or spiritual experience. They were not Western Europeans. Their worship, no doubt, included what they would describe as encounters with God and could be deeply emotional. On Pentecost, the outburst of tongues drew a crowd, some onlookers said the speakers were drunk! Did they look drunk? Did they stagger as they spoke in languages they could not understand? Who knows?

Paul took it as normal for believers to be encountered by God via the third person of the Trinity, the Holy Spirit. Jesus seems to be saying something similar in his treatment of the Spirit in John 14-16. Dr.

James D.G. Dunn helped me sort out my theology regarding how the Spirit brings us into experiential friendship with God in his book *Jesus and the Spirit*.[1]

> The Spirit is that power that operates on the heart of man—the 'heart' being the center of thought, feeling and willing, the center of personal consciousness, what we might call the experiencing I. ... the Spirit is that power of inner life which leaves far behind all the merely ritual and outward and makes faith in God and worship of God existentially real. (James D.G. Dunn, Jesus and the Spirit p.201, Westminster Press, Philadelphia.)

All this supported my Biblical understanding and my own experience in relating to God. I was freshly excited to know God and expected the Spirit to move me into a deeper friendship with the Father and the Son.

Swimming in the ocean requires a holistic engagement with God, and that includes knowing His care and affection and experiencing his empowerment up close and personal. If you are berating yourself because you have not had such an encounter, please stop. Most of us are in a long learning curve on the journey of experiential Christianity. I certainly am.

Finally, I'll suggest to you two things that have helped me continue the journey.

1. My expectation based on scripture is that God *wants* to encounter me. I believe this is the sort of intimate relationship Christ died to give us.

2. I stopped comparing my experience of God with others. All of us are encountered by the Lord *as we need to be*. To miss this point is to become

distraught and may even cause you to stop expecting altogether. The other extreme is to try so hard to experience God the experiences themselves become contrived. Take it easy.

QUESTIONS FOR REFLECTION AND DISCUSSION:

1. Do you have a personal relationship with God? Explain.

2. What are the barriers you encounter in pursuing an experiential relationship with God?

3. What things help you nurture a relationship with God?

4. What other thoughts or questions did the reading stir in you

END NOTES:

1. Dunn, James D.G. *Jesus and the Spirit*. Westminster Press. Philadelphia. 1979

SHAMELESS

Read Luke 8:40ff; 1 John 1:3-7.

J esus was on his way to pray for the adolescent daughter of a synagogue official who had died. A large entourage traveled with him, jostling and crowding him. During the trek to the official's house, a sick woman approached him.

The nature of the woman's affliction (bloody discharge) made her "unclean," excluding her from Temple or Synagogue worship. She was, in effect, barred from the center of Jewish life and community. She was a virtual outcast among her people.

Many in her culture believed sickness was a punishment from God for sin; her affliction aroused not only physical pain but emotional shame.

Presumably, she already knew she was far from perfect, as most sane people do, or maybe, she even shared the faulty belief system of her neighbors. If she did, was she only getting what she deserved? Was the God of Israel rejecting her too? Maybe she was indeed cursed.

None of the doctors to whom she'd paid all her money could help her. She did have a final hope, a long shot, but a hope, nonetheless. There was a young prophet, a rabbi, called Jesus who was also a healer.

The rumor was, Jesus "touched"—physically touched—"unclean" people—even lepers, and his touch healed them. Such reports emboldened her, and when she learned the young rabbi was coming near; she decided to approach him anonymously, cloaking herself in the crowd that surrounded him.

He was coming by; here was her chance. She pushed her way through his entourage and brushed the corner of his robe with an outstretched hand. Suddenly, warmth coursed through her body! Creeping back, she knew her suffering was over; her bleeding had stopped! But Jesus stopped too, and he called her out—in front of all her neighbors.

His disciples thought he was kidding, "Who touched me? Look, people everywhere and you can ask who touched me?"

But the woman who had tried to remain anonymous knew it was hopeless. She'd tried to stay in the shadows, but Jesus continued to persist, "Who touched me? I felt power go out of me."

Why did Jesus insist the woman go public? Many have pointed out she was publicly barred from community life; so, Jesus wanted to publicly restore her to ensure her acceptance back into the community, which sounds like something Jesus would do. But I think the Lord also wanted to accomplish something more. He wanted her to see, in His eyes, the love and acceptance of God.

I hadn't seen that in the story before and now, God was talking to me: "Barry, I wasn't ashamed of her, and I'm not ashamed of you. Look me in the eye; let me look at you."

That hit me hard, because I often feel unclean when I fail or even sometimes when I don't. Like the woman in the story, I want God's benefits, but I also want to remain anonymous—especially with my peers but also with God, as if such a thing were possible! When I feel unclean, I cannot bear looking into the eyes of Jesus.

But this is not the relationship God calls us to have with him or, for that matter, with our friends. He is the God who calls us out of darkness into his marvelous light. Staying in the light banishes shame.

The first epistle of John tells us how to do it in our relationship with God and each other.

> This is the message we have heard from him and declare to you: God is light, and in him is no darkness at all... if we walk in the light, as he is in the light, we have fellowship with one another and the blood of Jesus purifies us from all sin. (1 John 1:5-7)

My current practice is to take my shame directly to Jesus by regular repentance and confession. I also have a group of friends with whom I share my darkness, fear, and sin. They speak God's forgiveness to me and pray for me.

Jesus is not ashamed of us. Since my meditation on the story of the sneaky woman, I've stopped being sneaky with God and my faith family. On particularly "unclean" days, I no longer hide from Jesus, as Adam and Eve did in the garden. God wants to be with us, and I've decided to keep the door open on my side; shame is not in control anymore.

QUESTIONS FOR REFLECTION OR DISCUSSION:

1. Can you relate to the woman who wanted healing but also wanted to remain anonymous? Explain.

2. Is it easy or hard for you to look into Jesus' eyes?

3. Are you sometimes ashamed when you really should not be ashamed? If so, why?

4. What makes you feel unclean?

5. What did you learn from the passage in 1 John quoted above?

6. What other thoughts or questions did the reading stir in you?

STRANGE WATERS

"You've been leading me
beside strange waters
Streams of beautiful lights in the night
But where is my pastureland in these dark valleys?"
If I loose my grip, will I take flight?
"Strange Waters" Album, "The Charity of Night,"
– Bruce Cockburn[1]

Some authors and speakers describe life in the Spirit in terms of success—one miraculous event after another. My experience has been entirely different. Sometimes the Spirit has led me beside, not 'quiet waters' (Psalm 23), but as Bruce Cockburn sang, "Strange waters."

For two years of my life, I was depressed. I think now, it was clinical depression, but I could not admit it then. I was a pastor, and the joy of the Lord was my strength; how could I admit I was depressed? My response was "be happy"—but that simply spiraled me downward.

I also 'rebuked' the devil, but nothing changed. I'd wake up in the morning and feel as if the only thing I wanted to do was go back to bed. In those 24 months, I got Christian counseling, which was helpful, but the main thing I did was to stop fighting, accept what I was experiencing, and try to find God in the midst of it. I learned to stop asking, "Why, I'm a pastor, why me?" And I began asking, "What? What are we doing here Lord; what are you teaching me?"

I've come to believe the Spirit will bring us not only into the high places of victory, but also into trials to perfect us as Paul and James taught (Romans 5:3-5; James 1:2-4). Jesus, our model for how to live, was led into testing by the Spirit. Why should I escape? A sequence of events in Jesus' life helped me understand how this works.

Ironically, Jesus' testing occurs on the heels of a spiritual high. The high was his baptism by his cousin, John, in the Jordan River. The experience would be a wonderful affirmation of Jesus, not unlike what we might experience at a party in our honor or our graduation celebration upon completing high school or college. Jesus' baptism was an occasion that would launch him into his life of ministry.

Jesus' closest intimates were at the Jordan that day. There was, of course, John, the baptizer, and fellow kingdom conspirator. But there were unseen guests present, too. God the Father spoke the deepest affirmation to him, "This is my beloved Son, with him, I am well pleased." The Spirit descended upon him like a dove, a priceless graduation gift from his Father (Matthew 3:13-17; Mark 1:9-11; Luke 3:21-22).

As they were for the very human Jesus—these realities are absolute necessities for ocean swimmers—because after exiting the waters of baptism, Jesus would enter the "strange waters" of testing where the strength he gained and the affirmations he heard at his graduation party would sustain him as he faced the tests.

The same Spirit who saturated Jesus and affirmed to him the Father's love led him into the desert to be tempted by the devil. Mark puts it starkly: *"At once the Spirit sent him out into the desert, and he was in the desert for forty days, being tempted by Satan" (Mark 1:12).*

Some Greek scholars say the translation could have been, "...the Spirit 'drove' Jesus into the desert."

In the second movie of the original "Star Wars" trilogy, Luke Skywalker is exiled to a secluded place in the galaxy to be equipped by the Jedi master Yoda. Luke begins to learn the ways of the force, and the amazing things he can do in the power of the 'good side.' Luke soon believes he can do battle with the dark side and wants to try right away. Yoda warns him; "Reckless, you are. You'll ruin everything"! Luke answers, brashly, "I'm not afraid." Yoda's reply is soft but menacing, "You will be." After the warning, Skywalker ventures into a dark cave, where—encountering his deepest fears—folds, overwhelmed by the test.

The Spirit drew me into a cave of depression. There were things God wanted to teach me I could only learn there. I often wilted, even thought of giving up pastoring to find another line of work. Jesus did not need this sort of perfecting, but I did. I needed to become dependent on God rather than myself.

Needless to say, Jesus' testing was on a wildly higher plane than is ours. His experience, however, is still a paradigm for his followers for how the Spirit leads us, and how God makes us more like him.

Sometimes the Spirit leads us beside 'strange waters,' dark places. Perhaps this is why Jesus counseled us to pray: *"Lead us not into temptation (The test) but deliver us from the evil one" (Matthew 6:13).*

I once read an article by J.I. Packer on this petition. He affirmed that God often brings us into places that test our faith. He interprets the prayer from Jesus as acknowledging in humility that we are not really up to the test, "Lead us not…" This humility is the opposite of Luke Skywalker's, "I'm not afraid." But the second clause of the petition is, "but deliver us from the evil one." That is, "Oh God, don't lead me to the test. I know me, and I'll blow it. But, Lord, if you do lead me there, don't let the evil one destroy me or defame your work in me."

The Spirit-filled life includes suffering and pain as well as joy and comfort. Now, before I rebuke the devil when I'm in a hard place, I check in with God. What are we doing here Lord; what are you saying to me in this? Ocean swimming will always bring us into 'strange waters,' but there is life in the ocean. Jesus is there with you, and it's worth the risk.

QUESTIONS FOR REFLECTION AND DISCUSSION:

1. How does it make you feel knowing God sometimes leads us into testing?

2. When you are going through a hard time, what is your first inclination? Why?

3. Do you think all trouble is a test from God? Explain.

4. Do you see God leading you through life, or do you see yourself as the one who decides your direction?

5. What other thoughts or questions did the reading stir in you?

END NOTES:

1. Cockburn, Bruce. *Strange Waters*. The Charity of Night Album. Reaction Studios, Toronto. 1997

HEALING

M y wife and I had moved to Los Angeles so I could pursue, of all things, beach volleyball! We quickly discovered living near the beach was way out of our price range, so the volleyball thing faded too. But there we were in L.A. I got a job at an audio retail store selling speakers and receivers where I met many new friends; one of them was Harry.

Harry and I played one-on-one basketball every Saturday morning at a Catholic center in California's San Fernando Valley. He was a big guy from New York who fit all stereotypes. Loud, gruff and in your face, which was just the way he guarded me in our games; hands-on and pushy!

I drove around him to the hoop one morning, and he knocked me off balance as I went in for the layup. I came down awkwardly and rolled my left ankle underneath the rest of my leg, heard it pop and fell cursing on the blacktop. I had rolled that ankle many times before and knew I had a long rehab in store.

While writhing and cursing, I heard a voice that wasn't Harry's, "We couldn't help overhearing that you were hurt…" I looked up and saw two strangers peering down at my misery.

Standing behind them, shrugging his big shoulders, Harry rolled his eyes to let me know he had no idea what these guys were doing. Then the man doing the talking said, "Do you mind if we pray for you?" That was weird, but I knew about praying—my mom was a faithful Methodist, so I said sure, thinking it would get rid of these intruders.

But, no, he wanted to pray for me right then and there! When the man who was doing the talking asked if he could put his hand on my ankle, I was mildly shocked, who was this person? I heard myself saying 'ok' not knowing exactly why; maybe deep down I thought it just might work.

My unknown rescuer (I learned later he and his friend had been playing tennis on a nearby court) grabbed my ankle with both hands and started praying. The language he used was not English, but I reasoned, Catholic recreation center by a Catholic church, must be Latin. I was no rube, I knew Catholics loved Latin. What I could not have known then was he was speaking in what the Bible calls tongues, a spiritual gift.

He then said to my ankle (yes, to my ankle) in a commanding voice in English, "Be well! Inflammation, go!" After the strange prayer, he said, "Why not get up and see how it feels." But I knew how it would feel; I'd sprained my left ankle so frequently there was lumpy deformity present even when it was not injured. Nevertheless, for some reason, I decided to give walking a try.

I was shocked. There was little pain or swelling, my ankle felt ok, and I immediately felt foolish for having made such a big screaming, cursing deal out of an injury that apparently had not been that bad in the first place! I said to the praying guy and his sidekick, "Well, uh, I guess I didn't hurt it as bad as I thought." They just smiled, said, "God bless you," and headed back to their tennis game.

I won't repeat Harry's remarks here. Suffice to say he was incredulous, and we, both being from outside nutty California, chalked the experience up to "left-coast" weirdness. It was only after my conversion to Christianity that I recalled the incident. As I reflected on it, my eyes widened, and I said out loud, "Oh, God, that was you wasn't it?" Yes, it was. I was healed by Jesus through prayer before I believed in Jesus.

Jesus' healing ministry, so prevalent in the Gospels demonstrates a picture of the restoration of God's kingdom rule in the cosmos. When Jesus prayed prayers of 'command' such as, "be well" "be healed" "come out!" he demonstrated his authority over sickness and demonic oppression. And he did so not in the power of his deity but as a human filled with the power of the Spirit (Mark 14:36; John 5:19; Matthew 12:28; Acts 10:38; Philippians 2:8). He, therefore, becomes the model of a Spirit-filled person; the pattern of how disciples are supposed to continue His ministry via the Spirit (John 14:12-17; Acts 1:8).

Jesus' healings were proclamations of God's rule breaking into our fallen world, and Jesus intended His body, the church, to extend His ministry (Matthew 28:18-20; Luke 9:1-6; 10:1-3; John 14:12-14; 1 Corinthians 12-14). The tennis player who prayed for me all those years ago was continuing the ministry of Jesus.

God's goal is wholeness; everything broken will come back together in Jesus (Ephesians 1:9-10) and we get to play.

QUESTIONS FOR REFLECTION AND DISCUSSION:

1. Above, you have an outline of my views on Christian healing. What are yours?

2. In your opinion, why was physical healing a major part of the ministry of Jesus?

3. Have you ever seen God's kingdom come via physical healing? What happened?

4. What are the barriers Christ followers have to the ministry of physical healing today?

5. What other thoughts or questions did the reading stir in you?

CHURCHES AND BUILDINGS

I converted to Christianity in a little church called the Vineyard. In a few decades, the Vineyard movement would grow to about 1,500 local churches. But when my wife and I showed up, we were just one congregation of about 100 people meeting in a square dance hall near Los Angeles.

The place we rented was on the property of a Lutheran church. Our lease there was not renewed and sent our pastor scrambling to find us a meeting place. He thought he'd found one in the Samuel Wise Temple on Mulholland Drive just off Laurel Canyon Boulevard, because on Sunday mornings the temple was not in use. But the agreement fell through a weekend before we were to leave the Lutheran place. We were homeless.

Our pastor, Kenn, prayed and thought he heard God say we were supposed to meet at lifeguard station 13 on Santa Monica beach the next Sunday morning. My wife and I thought that sounded even cooler than the temple and eventually, we received water baptism in the stretch of the Pacific near lifeguard station 13.

Swimming in the ocean is always an adventure, and God's kingdom consists in seemingly uncanny and messy stuff. We met on the beach every Sunday for the next eight months, growing from about 100 to 800 members.

His back to the Pacific, our pastor used a portable loudspeaker hooked to an electric generator to amplify his voice as beach walkers on their morning stroll gawked at our odd gathering. What sort of group got up this early to go to the beach for a lecture?

One morning, a young man approached our pastor from behind, and to the shock of those of us listening, grabbed the mic from his hand and shouted, "You people are all brainwashed Lemmings! Why are you listening to this stuff?"(He did not use the word stuff.)

Kenn took the microphone back and asked the young man why he felt the way he did. They dialogued a bit in front of us, and I thought to myself, "I bet Jesus would do the same thing! Our pastor is showing concern for the guy who just interrupted his talk." I was impressed.

Their conversation did not last long as two of the larger members of the congregation showed up on Kenn's right and left. When the guy saw them, he sensed his time was up.

But there was no manhandling or shaming involved. The guys merely walked him away, presumably to continue the dialogue our pastor had started. Kenn turned to us and resumed preaching. I was proud of our church and our pastor that day.

A church with walls can certainly be a sanctuary where we renew each other in God. But what I learned that day on the beach early in my journey with Jesus is that church is supposed to be a dynamic force or as Jesus would say "Salt and Light" in the world.

Our walls protect us from controversy or danger similar to the protection we get from swimming in the pool. Using the metaphor of ocean swimming, when our church was gathering on the Pacific all those years ago, it felt like we were swimming together in the ocean, a church without walls.

QUESTIONS FOR REFLECTION AND DISCUSSION:

1. Do you usually identify the church as a building? Why or Why not?

2. Had you been speaking to the crowd at the beach, how would you have handled the young man who grabbed the mic from you?

3. Is it easy or hard for outsiders to break into your church? Explain.

4. What other thoughts or questions did the reading stir in you?

DISSATISFIED CUSTOMERS

A group of us often went to the local mall to pray for random people on Saturday mornings. Praying for strangers was mildly awkward, of course, but worth it when Jesus showed up too—and with very few exceptions—everyone we asked to pray for said, yes.

We even prayed for clerks and workers in the mall with the rule being not to disturb them if they were serving a customer. So, when I saw a young woman in an empty storefront one morning, I went in and began a conversation.

Not that it matters, but she was thoroughly tattooed and full of piercings, two-tone hair and dressed in black. She fit the decor of the alternative "new age" store she worked in well.

I said, "Hi, I'm from a local church, and on Saturdays, we come to the mall to pray for people, can I pray for you?" At this point in the conversation, the subject usually says something like, "Sure, I guess so or Ok." A few others might say, "Right here, now?" Here's what she said, "Don't you know the mall does not allow religious solicitation? I'm calling security right now!"

I was mildly shocked, having not heard a reply like this in our experience there, so I said, "No, I did not know. We have been doing this for a few years, and I've never heard it from anyone."

Then her pain started pouring out. She said, "I know you people; you act all 'lovey-dovey' and accepting but kick people to the curb who look a little different." Recovering a bit, (I think the Lord helped me to be slightly less defensive) I said, "Did that happen to you?"

"You bet it did," she shot back, "they were so mean I'll never go near a church again!"

The next thing I said, I'm pretty sure was from the Lord, too, because my rote response would have been to defend the church by saying something like, "Well, all churches aren't like that, why not give ours a chance." But I did not say that, I opened my mouth, and this is what came out:

"I am so sorry for the way the church treated you, and as a representative of the church, I ask you to please forgive us."

The expression on the young woman's face softened from hostile to vulnerable right before my eyes; tears appeared in the corners of her eyes and she said, with some difficulty, "No one from the church has ever said anything like that to me."

I would have pressed on from there but felt as if the Spirit said, "That's enough for now." I'm thankful for that prompting in light of all the times I have inappropriately pushed beyond what God was doing.

The next time we went to pray at the mall, I went straight to her shop, she wasn't there. I'd never gotten the name of the tattooed lady, but when I described her to the new clerk, she told me she had quit and moved on.

I occasionally pray for her, that God would bring her the next step back into his path. I suspect she did take a step toward God as I confessed the sins of the church she had personally experienced and asked her forgiveness.

Questions for Reflection and Discussion:

1. Have you encountered folks who are hostile toward the church? What happened?

2. Has the church alienated you? How?

3. How do you feel about confessing the corporate sins of the church?

4. What other thoughts or questions did the reading stir in you?

SIN

*"Some things last longer than you think they will
There are some kind of things you can never kill."
– Bob Dylan, "Cold Irons Bound."[1]*

The ocean is admittedly a dangerous place to swim. There are undertows and riptides galore, and one of them is Sin. Sin is destructive thinking and behavior. Sin is disobeying God and, of course, is practiced in both the pool and the ocean.

When I came into a conscious relationship with Jesus in 1976, I immediately stopped doing drugs, getting drunk, and being sexually promiscuous. My language changed, abruptly. All of this was amazing to me, and looking back, I can take little credit for exercising much "willpower" if any. I just felt free from pleasures that became slave drivers.

Imagine my distress when I found myself going down the same road again, 40 years later. Admittedly, not to the reckless extent I did before my conversion, but if I'm honest, the pathway looks eerily similar. I appreciate the Bible's teaching on no drunkenness, yet I sometimes drink too much.

I have also abused prescription pain drugs, by which I mean I occasionally took one when I could have done without it. Apparently, I was not through with chasing a buzz.

I struggle with other sins too, such as, greed, jealousy, coveting, judging others, and dishonesty. But my dalliance with prescription drugs and alcohol abuse seem especially hypocritical to me, because I've spent years preaching about how Jesus delivered me from those things and now found myself playing around with danger again.

The very idea I could be involved with this stuff seems, to me, more like betraying a friend than the violation of a rule. Intentional sin is a personal rejection of my friendship with God, and I hate it. Sadly, often, I don't hate it enough.

The point once again is this: Sin is betrayal, as well as rule breaking. Sin must always be taken personally, grieved over and confessed (1 John 1:9) to God and fellow swimmers (James 5:13-16). If you are not struggling with sin, you've deceived yourself (1 John 1:8). Your sin may not be as hypocritical and overt as mine, but I'd wager it is there just the same. Sin will catch up with you. Granted, I'm nowhere near the oblivion I experienced before my conversion but who am I fooling here, surely not God. At this writing, we are making progress again.

QUESTIONS FOR REFLECTION AND DISCUSSION:

1. What is your definition of sin?

2. What are some of the specific sins with which you struggle?

3. Do you have a friend who hears your confession and holds you accountable?

4. Do you agree with my statement above: "Sin is betrayal, as well as rule breaking?" Why or why not?

5. What other thoughts or questions does this reading stir in you?

END NOTES:

1. Dylan, Bob. *Cold Irons Bound.* Time Out of Mind Album. Special Rider Music. 1997

A MAN CALLED DEATH

Over the years I've come to understand, the person I think I am is more dependent upon the feedback of others than I ever knew. The problem is that the names and labels others hang around our necks are often false or seriously out of whack, especially when compared to what God says about us who bear his image.

A team of us deployed in Mozambique, Africa, some years ago to begin church planting efforts with locals in Gondola, a city on the eastern side of that country. Our hosts took us to do some ministry in a small prison where they regularly worked with the inmates.

On that particular day, our hosts had planned a water baptism, and our team pitched in by hiring a large plastic container hauled in by a truck one of our missionaries owned. There were ten or twelve young men who had said 'yes' to Christ in weeks past and wanted baptism. After preaching, that morning another dozen believed and wanted baptism, too.

In the dusty prison yard, we dipped a large pitcher into the container and poured the water of baptism over the heads of prisoners, who were publicly declaring their new-found freedom in Christ. The dust became mud as one man after another came under the cleansing flood. It was a glorious morning.

After the baptism, our team of six lined up facing each other and created a prayer tunnel of sorts so we could lay our hands on the guys and utter prayers of blessing as they slowly walked between us. Bonnie (another team member) and I stood at the end of the line ready to pray for the next man through. He couldn't have been much over eighteen.

Before we began to pray over him, Bonnie asked the man for his name. His answer, translated by one of our hosts got our attention—his given name was; "Death."

Later I discovered that tribal names like darkness and death were not uncommon in that part of the world, so, here was Death—staring us in the face.

The face did not look like death at all. The new convert looked hopeful, even joyous as if new life covered him. So, Bonnie renamed him on the spot. She said, "Your name is no longer Death. Today, Jesus says your new name is "Life."

As the translator relayed the young man's new name, a smile widened across "Death's" face and Death was no more; death had been "swallowed up in the victory" (1 Corinthians 15:54b). The victory Jesus won for us in his passion and resurrection.

I can't be sure if the young man we prayed for that day fully embraced his new identity, because there are many days I also fail to do so. But I do know he was renamed that day with a name that trumps any other hung around his neck before his baptism.

QUESTIONS FOR REFLECTION AND DISCUSSION:

1. What was your nickname as a kid? Did you like it or hate it?

2. What have others "told" you about who you are?

3. How does Christian baptism impact identity?

4. How have you held on to your new identity in Christ?

5. What other thoughts or questions did the reading stir in you?

INVISIBLE

M y wife, France, and I were converted a week apart back in 1976 at a Lutheran square dance hall, in the San Fernando Valley, rented by the small church plant we were attending called The Vineyard. France was converted a week before me, illustrating a familiar heel-dragging slowness on my part.

Thirty-five years later, my wife had a vision of what was happening in the unseen part of reality the day of her conversion. If you don't believe such things are authentically from God, what I'm about to share will not convince you, but I appeal to skeptics to suspend disbelief for the rest of this reading.

Here's how it happened:

She was participating in a guided meditation where the facilitator instructed the small group she was in to picture themselves riding in a car, with Jesus, on a beautiful spring day, windows down. They were then asked to listen to what Jesus might say to them.

France followed the plan and imagined Jesus sitting across from her in the back seat of a convertible, on a beautiful afternoon, and she heard the Lord say, "Do you know what happened the day you gave your heart to me?" France replied she did not.

Suddenly the scene changed, she and Jesus were together looking down upon that old Lutheran square dance hall in Van Nuys, California, where our church met. She described it as what she imagined an out-of-body-experience might be or, perhaps what the old skinflint Scrooge felt when the three Christmas ghosts took him flying into his past.

From above she saw us sitting, as usual in the front row, listening to Kenn, the pastor giving his weekly invitation to those who wished to trust Christ. The drill was to indicate you had said the "sinner's prayer" with Kenn by raising a hand. My wife saw her hand go up while I just sat there next to her. So far, so good, but what she saw next was shocking.

As we rose to leave, she saw heavy chains materialize and drop off her body. They fell to the floor; then dark things flew out of her, foul looking vapors flowed away from her ears and mouth, and dark clouds lifted from around her head.

She was clean. It took her breath away and left her in tears—Tears of joy. She wept and thanked Jesus profusely for showing her graphically what the New Testament promises to all converts. She now was even more convinced that what she believed had happened that day.

As Paul had it; she saw herself being "rescued from this current evil age, transferred from the kingdom of darkness to the kingdom of His dear Son" (Galatians 1:3-5).

She saw herself move from death to life.

Two things emerged as I reflected on her experience. First, there is a war raging. As one of my favorite songwriters, Marjorie Long has it.

"I can't ignore it anymore, there's a war, and I'm in the middle of it." She goes on:

"No more sleeping for me."

The writer is alive to the battle and prayer is a powerful weapon God gives to us to join him in contending for those who need deliverance. Often, right in the middle of a church service.

The war rages on two fronts. God is warring not merely with the "powers" who want to keep us in chains, but there is a battle inside those who are considering faith.

Anne Lamott commented on this inner conflict, and its lunacy: "I was not willing to give up a life of shame and failure without a fight."[1]

I picture sparks flying up from the pews as God's people pray for those in need of salvation in the audience; people God is drawing to Christ, who are not yet part of God's family.

Secondly, I thought about what might change if we got our arms around what went down at our own conversion? Would we live as people who have moved from the kingdom of darkness to the kingdom of light? Would there be new gratitude and more fervent worship? Would our self-perception alter when we think of who we are now in Christ?

I'm aware that conversion, for some, is an event they can date and talk about; for others conversion may be imperceptible except for the life changes that follow. What Jesus showed France pulled back the veil on the drama that goes on at regeneration, and I'll never forget it.

QUESTIONS FOR REFLECTION AND DISCUSSION:

1. What is your conversion story? Who was praying for you?

2. To what extent does praying for the salvation of others weigh into your regular practice of prayer?

3. Focus on Galatians 1:3-5. How have these verses played out in your own life? Explain.

4. What are your thoughts on the warfare aspect of the spiritual life? How would awareness of the "war" view change the way you pray and live?

5. What other thoughts or questions did the reading stir in you?

END NOTES:

1. Lamott, Anne. Traveling Mercies / Some Thoughts on Faith. Anchor Books Copyright 1999

Rudy

James, Jesus' half-brother, wrote that there should be no favoritism in church, but that hasn't stopped Christians from exalting some and ignoring others down through church history. In fact, the opposite is all too often true. (See James 2:1-4.)

Our church plant first met in a middle school gymnasium, which was freezing in winter and boiling with the infamous Midwestern humidity in the summer. Nevertheless, we were grateful to have space. The papers in the town dutifully did a little story about the new church plant, interviewed me and even printed my picture.

The article pointed out I had grown up in the little town in which we were planting and that our church was "non-denominational" which, in our conservative community, made us suspect. "Denomination" meant stability even if you disagreed with the theology of the denomination in question. It felt more secure to see a familiar name.

Our first Sunday morning was a frigid affair. I noted people left their coats on as they arrived since the gym was only slightly warmer than the weather outside. Stationed at the entry door with a few members of our planting team, I welcomed the curious and chilly folks to our first service. While I was chatting up a group of newcomers on what sort of church we were and answering their questions, a vaguely familiar-looking man trudged in the door, knocking snow from his knee-length rubber boots.

Rudy was a street person and former mail carrier who had undergone mild psychosis—if there is such a thing—apparently from taking too many hallucinogens. The reason he looked familiar was that I'd graduated kindergarten with Rudy, thirty-two years before! He called himself Bruce then and came across as a regular, likable kid. I still have a picture of our graduating class in front of a Methodist church building wearing our little mortarboards.

My former classmate was packed into three coats and a few sweaters, looking a bit like the Michelin tire man. Of course, homeless folks wear all they have all year round. He had a large set of keys hanging from his belt and a thick Sunday newspaper under his arm. His hat looked like something from "Nanook of the North," with flaps on both ears.

I maintained my eerie sense of recognition but just couldn't place him. He knew me before I remembered him—because of the news story—and took a long step toward the group I was trying to impress with how orthodox and safe our new church would be, even though we did not have a denominational name on the door.

As he strode toward us, Rudy said, very loudly, "Well I'll be damned!" He repeated the same shocking (for church) phrase even more loudly with each step!

He kept saying it until he reached us, and by the time I recognized my long-lost classmate, the folks I was conversing with had shrunk back.

I was facing a decision. Should I acknowledge that I knew this scraggly person or pat him on the back and send him toward the coffee pot? Now I'm ashamed at having had that thought, but hey I had a church to plant and a guy like Rudy, left– well– a certain scary impression on folks.

In the end, we embraced, and he said, "I'll be damned, the paper was right it is you!" Yep, it was me, and I don't think I ever saw any of the folks from the group I was speaking with at the door that morning again, but Rudy stayed and became a regular.

Not long after we left the gym, we rented an office building, a significant upgrade for our growing church. We had that space 24/7 and could do much more there. Rudy would come in on Sunday morning, the massive, clanging set of keys swinging on his belt like the chains of Marley's ghost in street person attire. He would stop at our little coffee bar, fill a supersize K-Mart cup with java, and load it with about ten packets of sugar.

Then he would jingle-jangle to his favorite seat in the front row and unfold his giant Sunday paper irritating all those behind him. Rudy was loud— snapping and straightening the pages of his reading material.

About ten minutes into my message, Rudy would leave his seat and jangle back to the coffee pot to fill up (which happened at least twice during the talk, sometimes three trips were made). At length, we lovingly asked him to sit in the back row (a direct violation of the text in James!), so he could be nearer the coffee, which made perfect sense to him.

Rudy attended our church on and off for about two years. A few of our folks befriended him, but he was shy of relationships. When he felt someone getting too close, he didn't show for a month. But I'm sure God loved Rudy through our church, and I know he loved us through Rudy.

Rudy disappeared after the first few years. Several of our members who got to know him searched, but no one was able to find him. But, over the years and mostly (I think) for our benefit, God would send us many more Rudy's. I'm ashamed to say we didn't always love them well. But for the most part, God kept us open, and we were the richer for it.

As we began our "Odyssey" in church planting, Rudy helped us a lot. You cannot choose the people God sends you to love. You can, of course, exclude or ignore them. Rudy reminded us that when it came to relating to God, we are all homeless people, albeit with better outer attire than Rudy. We conceal our broken hearts and damaged emotions, until Jesus begins to love us through his church. He wants to offer all and sundry coffee, a hug, and a family.

QUESTIONS FOR REFLECTION AND DISCUSSION:

1. Have you ever seen favoritism in church? Explain.

2. Have you ever felt excluded in church? Describe how it felt.

3. What are some ways we can welcome "Rudy's"?

4. Who are the Rudy's in your church, if there is none perhaps the question to ask is, why?

5. What other thoughts or questions did the reading stir in you?

READING 30

SHARKS

I was in Florida at my favorite spot, Plaza South,
when I got a call from my associate pastor. His
news was horrible; a church member and my close
personal friend, John, had been murdered in his own
home by an intruder. His wife, Susan, had found him in
a pool of blood.

The scene didn't happen in a so-called dangerous
area of town but in the "burbs"—where John (not his
real name) lived with his wife Susan (not her real name)
and their two young daughters—yet it had happened.

After the initial shock of receiving such news, I
took a walk on the beach. I was thinking of what I
could say at such a trauma laden memorial service.
What does a pastor talk about at a time like this?

In two days' time, I'd be home to officiate that
service. So, I walked, cried out to God and listened for
guidance, not realizing there was more shocking news
awaiting when I got home.

The morning of the service, I got a call from
another of John's close friends. He said he needed to
see me right away and a detective would be with him. A
detective? Why? My question went unanswered, but
they wanted to talk to me about John's murder. They

showed up a half hour later, and we sat down in my home office for a talk.

That morning I learned what law enforcement has always known; the spouse of a murder victim is often considered a suspect in the crime until proven otherwise. I also learned the detective was sure there had been an affair between John's wife, Susan, and a man who was remodeling their home. Police believed the lovers worked together to get rid of John, even hiring a "hit man" to accomplish their murderous scheme. I listened jaws agape in unbelief to the most sordid story I'd ever heard, and it involved trusted members of our church.

Sworn to silence about the content of our meeting, which took place about an hour before the memorial service I was to officiate, I became aware that I must just go through with the funeral as if I knew nothing. I felt helpless and angry.

In light of what I'd just heard, the scene at our church auditorium seemed surreal. In the front row, Susan and her two small girls, dressed in black; she with a veil over her face looking in every way the aggrieved wife.

Feelings of grief for the family, especially the kids rushed to the front of my brain, but the hardest part was summoning the strength to give Susan the benefit of the doubt, as she sat there in (mock?) grief. I plowed through that service, play acting as it were, dreading what I must do when it was over.

After the memorial, I asked Susan to accompany me into a side room of the church. When we sat down, I asked her if she had anything to do with John's murder. She would only say, "The truth will come out." She did not say, "I had nothing to do with it."

Later it was demonstrated that she was there when her husband was bludgeoned and shot in the head. Disgusted, I thought this finding couldn't be accurate. But it was, and Susan went to the penitentiary along with her lover and the hit man.

After she was sentenced, I visited her; she asked for baptism. The prison staff arranged it, Susan confessing her sins but never fully acknowledging what took place on that horrible summer night.

John and Susan were leaders in our church. John was a workout partner and close friend. My wife and I had been to dinner at their home and they at ours. All that and we didn't know them. What if we had invested more time? I decided our church had to get better at relationships and initiated a more demanding discipleship model.

The human heart is a vast territory and sadly unknown even to the person to whom it belongs. More demanding discipleship, notwithstanding, people looking at us from the outside seldom see into our hearts—unless the discipleship includes components of rigorous self-inventory, discovery and revelatory gifts, because only God and we have access to those remote places.

I am not sure such aggressive self-search would be tolerated, much less desired by most churchgoers today. Nor am I sure it would have prevented the tragedy described above, but we can surely do better to know and be known.

Finally, this story is a clear rebuke to much current thinking on why people do horrific things. No doubt some can be chalked up as mentally ill, but Susan was not anything of the kind. She was coldly rational and selfish to the extremity of murdering her husband. Sadly, evil is alive and working via human sin.

QUESTIONS FOR REFLECTION OR DISCUSSION:

1. Have you been shocked at the behavior of people you thought you knew? Explain. (If you are in a group do not mention names.)

2. What are your views on evil human behavior? Is it a real thing or merely a sign of mental illness?

3. How does the Biblical remedy for bad behavior (repentance, confession, restitution, and grace from God to avoid future sin) differ from a solely therapeutic approach? Can both be helpful?

4. How can the church help us know each other more deeply? Would people in your church tolerate such practices? Would you?

5. What other thoughts or questions did the reading stir in you?

"Do You Love Me?"

A dolescence is fraught with mental, emotional and physical change that engendered insecurity in most of us. When I was 13, an incident took place that took in all of the above.

My Father was the strong silent type, like a Gary Cooper character in the movies. (Google him) He provided and protected and made us proud, but none of his five kids had a keen sense of tenderness or affection from dad—which is not an uncommon story for kids of parents from the WWII generation. Our fathers seemed to have gone to different schools with the same curriculum.

Dad decided I would not be allowed to go out for the freshman football team. He did not trust the coaches or their methods because two of my older brothers suffered knee injuries in the program. Dad's decision seemed cruel to me; so impulsively, I found one of my miscreant friends, and we ran away from home.

We were gone two days and one long night. Our parents were worried to death while we were smoking cigarettes and hiding out—first in the announcer's booth of the high school football field, then on the roof of our town's pharmacy. On the second day, my friend's mom found us walking down the street in broad daylight; I guess by then we were ready to go home.

When I faced my parents, I did not get the storm of anger and punishment I expected. I got tears and love. (Later, the storm broke!) After the discipline I received, I found out what my father and brother-in-law had been doing while I was missing; they'd been searching. In fact, they had looked all night, traveling six hours south based on well-meaning but erroneous tips about two adolescent boys hitch-hiking down the freeway.

When I discovered what my dad had done, I felt ashamed for all the trouble and grief I'd caused. I also felt something else. It was the inner warmth of knowing I was loved. Dad did not talk much about his love, but what he did that night powerfully showed his love to a confused adolescent boy.

In the magisterial prelude to John's gospel we read: "In the beginning was the Word and the Word was with God and the Word was God" (John 1:1).

Then a bit further down John tells us what God the Father did through his Son, Jesus.

"The Word became flesh and made his dwelling among us" (John 1:14a).

God did not remain in the ivory tower of heaven and call down to us about his love. As my father came in search of me when I was an insecure kid, God also came to us in Christ. God's journey travels from infinite to finite from heaven to earth. And after he came, he died to redeem us on Calvary. Next time you are insecure about his love, remember, he didn't just throw down words of love, he came.

QUESTIONS FOR REFLECTION AND DISCUSSION:

1. Were you always secure in the love of your parents? Explain.

2. What about God's love for you? Do you feel secure in God's love?

3. What causes we humans to question God's love for us?

4. If you are a parent, what are some of the implications of today's reading?

5. What other thoughts or questions did the reading stir in you?

BE CAREFUL WHAT YOU ASK FOR

After Jesus rose from the dead and before Pentecost forty days later, there was a casting of lots to decide who would take the place of Judas, the Lord's betrayer who committed suicide. This would bring their number back to twelve.

The number twelve was significant because the apostles correspond to the twelve tribes of the New Israel Jesus was instituting called the church. Twelve were needed. The lot fell to Matthias.

Joseph Barsabbas, the other candidate, was not to be chosen. The passage says Barsabbas had been with the little band of believers, "the whole time the Lord Jesus went in and out among us." He was, so to speak, one of those on the ground floor of the Christian enterprise. I wonder how being passed over felt for him? Was he disappointed God did not see him as good enough? Perhaps.

On the other hand, tradition indicates all of the twelve, save John, died for their faith in Christ as if they had targets on their backs. Maybe being chosen is not all it's cracked up to be? God picked Abraham, then Israel, and we know how that turned out. A history of failure, exile, unprecedented persecution by Christians accusing Jews as Christ-killers, all capped off by the Holocaust. Lovely. Reb Tevia's line in the play "Fiddler on the Roof" comes to mind: "Lord I know we are the chosen people, but just once, could you choose someone else?"[1]

I'm a member of a Christian tribe called the Vineyard. When the movement was just getting started, John Wimber, our founding national director, told a group of us "wannabe" pastors and church planters, "If you can do anything else, by all means, do it."

What a strange thing to say to a group of potential leaders at the beginning of a new movement. Had I been the leader of a group just getting off the ground, I'd have been actively recruiting and inviting potential leaders into the world-changing possibilities God had for us, rather than making some lame appeal to reconsider committing to the cause. Either John was engaging in some bizarre reverse psychology, or he knew something his eager audience didn't. After forty years in the Vineyard movement, I'm pretty sure it was the latter.

Men and women want things. We want to matter and be accepted; to be loved just as we are. God offers all of us these things in abundance. God also invites us into a new community, called the church, where we can experience all of the above with and through other human beings—provided the church is functioning as it should.

But women and men also want other things. We want fame, platform, adulation; we want power and control over other humans. Our motives for desiring leadership in the church can be immature, unhealthy, and destructive—to ourselves and the church.

Perhaps, that is one reason the prophet Jeremiah said to his servant, "Do you desire great things for yourself? Do not desire them" (Jeremiah 45:5).

I don't know if Joseph Barsabbas was crestfallen when the lot fell to Matthias. He could have been at perfect peace, believing whatever God decided was best.

The reality is, those who desire fame, power, and so on in ministry can scarcely comprehend what they are asking for. There is a cost; leading in the church also involves sacrifice; think of the twelve and how they ended up. John Wimber's point in Palm Springs all those years ago makes perfect sense. Only embark on the path of a pastor if you can do nothing else. There are plenty of ways to serve the Lord, but pastoring God's people is a "calling."

For the longest time, I did not even have a definite sense God had chosen me. I just knew I couldn't do anything else. Along the way for the past thirty-five years, God has made substantial inroads in my soul, burning away a score of toxic motives. His laser continues to this day. Had I known what lay before me that day in Palm Springs, I may have chosen differently. But, thank God, I couldn't do anything else.

QUESTIONS FOR REFLECTION AND DISCUSSION:

1. Does the reading put you off from pursuing Christian leadership? Explain.

2. In your view, why did John Wimber discourage those who wanted to be church planters and pastors when the Vineyard was getting started?

3. What sort of leadership has God called you to in the church? What was your process for accepting the call?

4. What other thoughts or questions did the reading stir in you?

END NOTES:

1. Stein, Joseph. *Fiddler on the Roof.* 1971

WIRED FOR PRAYER?

In his classic book, *Celebration of Discipline,* Richard Foster wrote that: "(Prayer) is original research in unexplored territory." *(Celebration of Discipline pp. 40)[1]*

I always liked that statement because research assumes ongoing discovery not arriving at some ultimate destination. That's prayer. No matter how much I read and learn about it, there is more to know and experience.

Prayer as a requirement for ocean swimming seems obvious, yet believers spend little time at it according to survey data. I read an article many years ago that claimed the average Christian pastor prayed about 5 minutes per day. I don't think long prayer times are necessarily best, but 5 minutes? That might get them by in the pool but not the ocean.

So much has been written by spiritual masters on prayer that I consider myself a minnow, or maybe a one-celled ameba even though I spend more time in prayer than any other discipline. But there is one thing I'm pretty sure of; the best way to learn to pray is by praying.

As a young person praying, for me, was little more than rubbing Aladdin's Lamp than interacting with

God. My older brother, three years my senior (I was twelve at the time) told me, if I "really believed," God would give me anything I asked. I asked to grow to be six foot five inches tall, the height of my hero, University of Cincinnati and later NBA star, Oscar Robertson. I prayed that prayer for months, maybe years. I believed I had the talent, I just needed the height, but alas, I developed neither. When it became evident to me there was an indefinite postponement of the answer to my prayer, I gave up actively praying, unless, I was in trouble, which was most of the time.

Praying took on an entirely new meaning when Jesus rescued me twenty years later. It began to dawn on me that prayer wasn't about me at all, but about God and his kingdom. I don't mean I didn't ask for personal help. I mean praying became a way to know God, be known by God, and participate in the mission of the kingdom of God. All my mentors stressed the regular practice of prayer as essential. Daily prayer has been my habit ever since. If I don't pray during the day, I feel almost as if I haven't eaten.

Sometimes my prayers get very dry, like eating unbuttered toast. So, along with many of my friends, I have discovered it's ok to use the prayers of others to express my love for God and make my requests. Hundreds of prayer books are now available as Protestants rediscover how to use the written prayers of others. But the Bible itself is the best source of prayer materials, especially the Psalms.

When I'm falling asleep during prayer, or my head is spinning with distraction, I write my prayers to keep me focused. All of the above is old news, but good news for people who are figuring out how to swim in the ocean. Ocean swimming without heartfelt focused praying is impossible.

My friend Ken Wilson wrote a great book about praying called, *Mystically Wired,* which describes prayer as "going someplace."[2] That is, in praying we move into the realm of God, his kingdom reality. This sort of prayer can be a dramatic experience, but other times, like entering a familiar space and sitting down in a favorite chair.

Getting to that place can also be frustrating for impatient people like me but, remember—"It all counts" (See Reading 10)—because whatever your experience might be, God is with you and you are with God.

Ken's title, *Mystically Wired*, also suggests humans are created to interact with their creator. Neuroscientists like, Andrew Newberg, have "mapped" and measured what happened in the brains of Carmelite nuns as they were meditating. Newberg, observed, the part of their brains that helped them distinguish themselves from the rest of the world showed decreased activity or blood flow. This area is labeled the "orientation association area." But when this area "went dark" another area, called the "attention association area" lit up. The "attention association area" is active when we focus or concentrate, intently on one thing for an extended period. The "attention association area" of the brain "lit up" when the sisters were in focused meditation.[3]

Focused prayer can change how we experience reality. Our awareness of being separate from the world diminishes. Ken Wilson's description is helpful: *"... you experience a blurring of the boundary between you and that which is not you. (Mystically Wired, pp. 375)[4]*

The person intently, praying, meditating or worshipping can experience what researchers call a "Unitive Experience." This language sounds similar to the talk on the street used by psychotropic drug users in my hippie days: "becoming one with the universe." Could LSD or peyote stimulate the brain to mimic the effect of prayer or worship? I have no idea.

One name being used for the sort of research Andrew Newberg is doing is, "neurotheology." A perception emerges in the praying subject that transcends ordinary reality and catches them up in a transcendent or different sort of experience. That is, as Ken says, they "go somewhere." The question then becomes, if humans are wired to engage in higher unified reality, does it follow that such reality exists?

My materialist friends would say no so-called neurotheology is really about how the impersonal process of evolution—via natural selection—evolved the human brain with a capacity to reach beyond itself to somehow give us hope, which gave us a better chance at survival. To put the idea in a cruder way, we created our creator.

Some theologians say our physiological makeup has nothing to do with our spirituality in any measurable way. But the idea that our brains seem "set up" to experience such perception points move theists like me to say, "Of course, God hard-wired me to have a relationship with him. We are mystically wired."

I've learned just enough about this stuff to make me dangerous. I'm a pastor, not a scientist nor theologian, but I have "gone there." That is, I've experienced a love apart from myself not merely during meditation, but personal and corporate worship and prayer. Like going someplace and coming back to self-awareness. It's similar to the experience of losing one's self while viewing a vast writhing ocean or getting caught up in a great piece of music and coming again to self-awareness. You go somewhere; then you're back. My current amateurish view is that my God-given brain contains the hardware to process a relationship with God.

None of this is to say, those of us who pray have such an experience every time we meditate, pray, or worship. Nor do I mean to imply prayer without such perception is inferior or somehow not authentic. Jesus commands us to live in prayer regardless of "experience" of any sort. In fact, this often-mundane sort of prayer, IS in my view a compelling way of cooperating with God as he saves the world! And, as I mentioned above, some theologians say our physiological makeup has nothing to do with our spirituality in any measurable way. But isn't the possibility fascinating?

It may be that neuroscientists are plumbing another example of how science and faith are partners rather than enemies. Rabbi Jonathan Sacks wrote, "Science takes things apart to see how they work, faith puts things together to see what they mean." (*The Great Partnership*, Jonathan Sacks)[5]

QUESTIONS FOR REFLECTION AND DISCUSSION:

1. Describe how you thought about prayer when you were growing up. How have those views changed?

2. What are your thoughts on science and religion? Explain.

3. What do you think about the possible connection of how humans are "wired" and prayer? Explain.

4. Does this reading encourage you to pray more frequently? Why or why not?

5. What other thoughts or questions did the reading stir in you?

End Notes:

1. Foster, Richard. *Celebration of Discipline. Harper. San Francisco. 1998.*

2. *Wilson, Ken. Mystically Wired. Thomas Nelson Inc. 2009.*

3. *Newburg, Andrew. How God Changes Your Brain. Ballantine Books. 2010.*

4. *Wilson, Ken. Mystically Wired. Thomas Nelson Inc. 2009.*

5. Sacks, Jonathan. The Great Partnership. Schocken. 2011

BEYOND RESCUE

I once heard John Piper, an author/pastor from Minnesota describe a fantasy drama of being lost then found. I'll share what I remember from his word picture then paint an extra piece myself to depict what I believe is a more robust view of what salvation means for us.

Imagine yourself on a snowy mountainside; temperatures are sub-zero; you've lost your way, slowly hyperthermia is creeping into your body. The hope of rescue is ebbing away when you spot what appears to be light over the next set of craggy rocks. Struggling to the summit, you behold to your great joy and relief, the source of the flash you'd just glimpsed above the ridge. It was streaming through the windows of the most massive log lodge you had ever seen. Long plumes of smoke curled from a dozen immense rock chimneys on the roof; you can't suppress a laugh as you hurry down the ledges toward the door.

Your frostbitten fingers, too stiff to make a fist for knocking, slap at the door; you ignore the pain, glad beyond hope to be alive. The thick wooden portal swings open, luscious, almost blinding light pours out illuminating your frozen face. From within, a hearty laugh, followed by an invitation: "Come in! Be welcomed stranger; warm your bones." Joy-tears flood your eyes; you will not die, but live!

Piper's story captures nicely the pain of being lost without hope and rescued beyond all hope by Jesus. Now, as stated above, may I suggest an addition to his picture that goes further than rescue?

When stepping into the entryway of the lodge from the deathly cold, your mind is imprinted with the joy of just being alive. Then came the spoken invitation; "Come in, come in be welcomed, stranger, warm your bones!"

Humble, grateful acceptance of respite from the storm should be enough, right? But, now, listen more carefully. When you do, you will hear singing, laughing, coffee cups tinkling and animated storytelling. Listen: the same joyous booming voice that invited you into the house calls you beyond the entryway toward the heart of the roomy lodge.

You are invited further up and further in (as C.S. Lewis once put it) to the Great Room of the King, where the roaring fire crackles in a giant hearth and delicious smells of freshly baked scones permeate the atmosphere. God the Father calls you and me into the place where he holds forth with his family. A spacious but somehow cozy place, where the fullness of joy, healing, friendship, and enlightenment commingle. One might say it's like heaven, but we must remember heaven has invaded earth.

The Father not only saves us through Jesus Christ, he also invites us to intimacy in Christ. But, like the rescued person in Piper's story, we are often content just to be alive. We make our camp in the entryway of the lodge. I believe this grieves the heart of the Lord of the house since he knows if we come into his Presence regularly, especially in the company of his other children, we are saved to "the uttermost" as the old King James has it.

There is something else. Being God's friend also assumes we are called to participate in mission with King Jesus. The Great Room of warmth and relational intimacy with God and his people is not merely about healing fellowship. It's also a War Room, where the General equips his soldiers with weapons of love and justice assigning them to duty. We come into God's family for a missional purpose, caught up in the loving energy of the Triune God as he saves the world by sacrificial love.

Effective ocean swimming requires being with God in his Great Room. "Better is one day in your courts than thousands elsewhere" (Psalm 84:10a).

QUESTIONS FOR REFLECTION AND DISCUSSION:

1. How has God rescued you? Specifically, from what have you been saved?

2. If you have come into the Father's house from the "storm of judgment," where would you say you were now in The Father's house? (Entryway, The Great Room, other, explain.)

3. If you spend none or little time in "God's Great Room," how can you cooperate with The Father's invitation to come closer?

4. Is the place of intimacy also an appropriate War Room? Why, or why not?

5. What other thoughts or questions did the reading stir in you?

READING 35

STRONG

We become better ocean swimmers as God sculpts our hearts to receive new depths of what it means to be human. My young humanity was changed by a Pop Warner football coach named Harlan Strong circa 1963. I began playing for Coach Strong at age 8 and was a five-year veteran at 13. The coach forged championship teams, but more significantly: strong (pun intended) character in every boy he coached.

The year 1963 started badly for me. After playing football with the same guys for five years, my Dad (for good reasons I couldn't see at the time) refused to let me try out for the freshman football team at our high school. I was devastated. I felt invisible, left behind.

A perceptive reader of boys, Coach Strong saw my pain, and one fall day as I was watching his team practice, he casually walked over and asked me if I wanted to help coach. Me? An assistant? I can't explain what a gap his offer filled in my young life. My funk was over; Coach instinctively knew what I needed; he was a master. In that year of my so-called "assistant coaching," Harlan Strong modeled one of the most important lessons I ever learned on how to swim in the ocean.

Our team had won the local championship and been asked to travel to a "bowl game" in far-away Texas. Thirty players, our small coaching staff, and assorted parents traveled for twenty hours on a tour bus to San Antonio. We lost a hard-fought game to a good team, and tails between our legs, began the long journey home.

A freak snowstorm marooned us in Meridian, Mississippi, scattering Coach Strong and the parents from the bus station to search out lodging. The search proved unsuccessful, not because rooms were not available, but because our team included three black players. Remember, it was the Deep South in 1963.

For context, in the early '60s, racism was not only tolerated by "good Christian people" but justified based on stilted readings of Holy Scripture. Such readings were a sickening throwback to 19th-century interpretations favored by Southern preachers attempting to preserve a "way of life." A way of life most Southern whites longed to continue and blacks wanted to end.

The phrase "White Privilege" didn't exist, and kids like me were blissfully naive to its reality. At the same general time we were traveling back home from Texas, the Southern block of the U.S. Senate was thwarting so-called "Liberal" civil rights legislation which most Northern Senators were none too keen on either. Status Quo was the name of the game when it came to civil rights in 1963.

Even today, the poisonous root of racism produces its hateful fruit, but in 1963 it was so much worse. Thank God we've made some progress.

When the team learned we would not be put up in a motel to sleep between clean sheets on soft beds, but instead, be delivered into the Meridian, Mississippi, courthouse to sleep en masse on the floor of the city's courtroom, we were confused. We asked questions. Did the adults not have enough money?

The explanation was not shared with the team, but the coaches and parents knew the real reason there was no vacancy in Meridian that night. The motel owners operated on the "Jim Crow" system. Blacks and whites were separated in motels, restaurants, drinking fountains, restrooms and so on. Coach Strong, true to his name, refused such an arrangement saying, "If one of us were refused service at your places of lodging, none of us would patronize them." He said, we are a team and we would stick together.

Later, I learned that after the meeting with a few of the motel operators, Coach Strong called the City police and informed them since the snow storm forced us to stay in Meridian, it was their responsibility to put all thirty-eight of us up for the night.

I vividly recall two things. One, at 13, I thought it was cool to see the inside of a real courtroom, judge's dais, jury box, etc. But as an adult, I often think of our lodging that night as a bitter irony. The "Seat of Justice" being used to cover up injustice. Such a move, while not novel, is still sickening.

The second thing I remember was, for the first time in my life, I was entertaining the question, "why?" Why could my teammates not stay with us at a motel? Sure, I knew the difference between black and white; I vaguely felt the stigma, the separation. How could I escape it; I lived in Kentucky in 1963. But when I asked "why" on that night, the blatant injustice of the event became real to me and hit me full force.

The events in Meridian were a lot for me to take in at 13, but my experience did not come near the horrid realities to come for the black boys on our team.

Injustice would be their regular diet for the foreseeable future, and but for people like Harlan Strong, even worse.

Because of Coach Strong's stand and appreciation for my black teammates, I could no longer blissfully ignore injustice. Coach's insistence on including them and his no-compromise demands upon city authorities in the Deep South at a time when it was unpopular and even dangerous left a permanent impression on me. Harlan Strong shaped the way I think about race relations and justice today. Through him, God sculpted me into a better human being and a better ocean swimmer.

QUESTIONS FOR REFLECTION AND DISCUSSION:

1. As you grew up, did you have people in your life like my Coach Harlan Strong? Name them.

2. What are a few significant life lessons you learned from your mentors?

3. The story above highlights race relations. Who or what has shaped your views on this significant subject? Explain.

4. To whom are you a Harlan Strong? If no one, to whom could you offer such a relationship?

5. What other thoughts or questions did the reading stir in you?

A SATISFIED MIND

I t is an established fact that Americans use anti-depressants in record numbers. An opioid crisis is raging at every level of our population. Why are people so sad? Why? While many answers are on offer for such questions, one answer, for sure, is we don't understand contentment.

Contentment is neither the giddy thrills of happiness nor defeated depressed surrender. It is an inner attitude of the heart, which preserves joy and peace regardless of the circumstances of life. Contentment is essential for an ocean swimmer. Without it, we drown—usually in endless striving or self-pity.

I met a remarkable man called, Benji, in the seaside resort of Pemba, Mozambique, while on a short-term mission trip. A mission partner and I went ahead of our primary team to conduct meetings there when a scheduling glitch left an entire group of people who had traveled a long way waiting for a speaker. Benji talked with broken English, but without saying a word, he taught me a memorable lesson on what contentment looks like in human life.

My colleague and I were to stay at a beach home owned by full-time missionaries who spent part of the year living and working there. I use the phrase "beach home" loosely, as it was nothing fancy—a small one bedroom on the Indian Ocean, complete with massive geckos on the ceiling and giant millipedes in the shower to greet us. In Mozambique, if you had a house, a wall was required, usually with razor wire spiraled around the top to discourage intruders. Benji was the guard, caretaker, gatekeeper—spending most days and nights on duty.

He lived in a small hut at the gate of the house. I got a look at the inside of his quarters as I came into the compound. It was about eight by eight, barely enough to accommodate his tiny bed and a small gridiron stove for warmth and cooking. There were no indoor facilities.

When we arrived, Benji greeted us with a big, toothy smile that never seemed to leave his lips. He helped us get settled, clearing away most of the geckos stuck to the ceiling, arranging mosquito nets over our beds and telling us how to navigate the local environment.

Benji and I talked together for a time that afternoon, and I learned he had a wife and four children. A bit shocked, I enquired how often he got to sleep at home. Every other weekend when the other guard was on duty, he said. Was it hard for him to be away from his family so much? Oh, no, he told me, through his sunny smile; he was thanking Jesus every day for a job, as most of his friends and family had none.

Later, when I lay down for the evening, staring at the wildlife that had returned to the ceiling, I felt sad for Benji, a middle-aged man with absolutely no hope of making progress to a better life. He would always be a doorman living in a hut to keep his family alive. I mused on the privilege of being born a United States citizen and thanked God for it. I also remember feeling guilty about having so much when Benji had so little. Of course, I would get over the thought and resume my privilege without much ado. But for an interruption.

"Why do you feel sorry for Benji?" The question came into my head unbidden. I've learned this sort of intersecting thought is often God speaking. More ideas poured into my mind. I remembered the earlier conversation I had with the cheerful doorkeeper. We talked about Jesus and what he meant to us, and Benji's part of the discussion was full of a joy I didn't often detect in myself or most of my U.S. friends. He was animated, grateful and sold out to Jesus.

Benji was content.

How was this possible? He was undoubtedly grateful for what he had. What did he have? The basics, food, clothes work and a loving family (1 Timothy 6:6-10). Perhaps he did not know he needed all the stuff Americans think they need to find happiness?

Benji will probably always be a doorkeeper; without a color TV, indoor toilet and a host of other things we in America call necessities. He is, after all, a doorkeeper in a disadvantaged country but also in the house of the Lord. (See Psalm 84.) That is, he lives in God's presence, and God has blessed him with what he needs.

When Paul wrote about contentment to the Philippian church, he let them know he had found a secret, producing in him contentment no matter what life threw at him. How? He said it was Christ who strengthened him (Philippians 4:10-13).

But what does that mean? It means he was at rest in God during circumstances beyond his control. He would rejoice in God in times of blessing and trust in times of trouble. Benji, like Paul before him, had Christ on board. The Presence is the secret.

The Apostle Paul endured unjust imprisonment, starvation, stoning, and shipwreck. His inner peace held even in the worst of times. But there is something else tucked away in Paul's teaching that Americans need, desperately to see, but often miss. "I have learned to be content in every situation…" That is, not only bad times but also in good times, times of "plenty."

Affluence is not an issue Benji will face, but you and I will. Why would contentment be threatened by good times? Could it be that those who enjoy "plenty" are in constant danger of confusing stuff with God? If a little is good, more must be better. And when more doesn't deliver, we find ourselves pushing the boundaries of pleasure into oblivion (the opioid crisis) or stuck in the throes of sadness (millions of Americans on anti-depressants). We are like people sickened from gorging too much cake.

I felt sorry for the middle-aged doorkeeper, but my sorrow was misplaced; he is fine. For Benji and Paul before him, God's presence was enough—preserving peace and joy, in good times and bad.

QUESTIONS FOR REFLECTION AND DISCUSSION:

1. Do you know anyone like Benji in the United States? Reflect on their lives. How does their thinking and lifestyle differ from yours?

2. Some writers contrast what we call happiness with contentment. How would you distinguish the two?

3. What attitude changes would you need to make to be like Benji?

4. What challenges to contentment are presented by having "plenty"?

5. What other thoughts or questions did the reading stir in you?

READING 37

A TIME FOR EVERYTHING

Mark Twain was famous for using earthy, humorous illustrations to sharpen the point he was making. I'm no Mark Twain, but below I'll attempt to do the same to illustrate a lesson all ocean swimmers need to learn.

My girlfriend's father owned a boat he docked on the (then and still) polluted Ohio River near Cincinnati. They were all water skiers, but I had never tried the sport. I was shy of trying to ski, who wants to look bad at 15? Nevertheless, one afternoon they talked me into being pulled along behind the massive twin Mercury engines attached to their pleasure craft.

The Mercs had so much torque getting up on the skies was a cinch, so far, so good; I was skiing! We picked up speed quickly, and I was having a blast, thinking, hey, I'm pretty good for a beginner. But when we swung around to head back toward the dock, I began to lose my balance and fall.

Maybe I did not want to look bad, or perhaps I thought I could pull myself back up on the skis, I don't know. But instead of letting go of the handle at the end of the ski rope, I held on. The result was very unpleasant. I got a dirty Ohio River enema in exchange for not turning loose of the handle. Did I mention the story was earthy? The enduring lesson for ocean swimmers is: letting go is sometimes the best policy.

When I decide to give up on never giving up, I make a statement about my future. Namely, God may have more productive options for me to pursue. Knowing when to "fold 'em" is an essential skill for ocean swimming.

Solomon told us there was a time for everything, and while he does not mention letting go, "everything" assumes it (Ecclesiastes 3:1-8).

Don't misunderstand. I'm not advocating becoming a "quitter." There are things we should never give up on, like a hard marriage (unless abuse, abandonment. or adultery is present; even then, divorce may or may not be the best choice) or trusting God even when life stinks.

Faithful perseverance is the operative phrase for the ocean swimmer in these and many other cases.

But holding to a course that is doomed, out of pride or prolonging a career choice that is sucking the life from your soul, is worse than an Ohio River enema. Below are a few boilerplate examples of things we really should turn loose.

Bitterness and unforgiveness: Some of us hold, with fierce tenacity, the right to hate and punish those who hurt us rather than forgive them. Bad idea, as most Christ-followers know, unforgiveness always comes back to bite us (Matthew 18:21-35).

Safety: After our hearts are shattered by people we love, we close them off for fear of more hurt in the name of safety. Sadly, such security is only available in a mausoleum.

Destructive attitudes: When we persist in holding to corrosive ideas like racism, classism or sexism, they will surely fill us with poison like the polluted water of the Ohio River filled me all those years ago.

Past achievements: Resting on laurels is always a bad idea. Such living may feel comfortable, but it slams the door on what God wants to do in us and through us today and tomorrow (Philippians 3:12-16).

The small sample above represents the sort of stuff an ocean swimmer must let go. Not releasing such things will be poison and unpleasant like my water-skiing adventure. God has something better for us when we learn how to be perceptive quitters.

QUESTIONS FOR REFLECTION AND DISCUSSION:

1. Think of a time when you should have quit but did not. What happened?

2. What are some hard things to which you believe you must hold? Why do you feel that way? How can the church help?

3. Is God prompting you to let go of an attitude, career choice, corrosive habit, or something else? Name it, then decide how you will let it go.

4. What other thoughts or questions did the reading stir in you?

RISING TOGETHER

P salms 120-134 are called songs of ascents. They evoke a picture of Israelites caravanning together up to Zion (Jerusalem) to one of the three major feasts God gave Moses to memorialize God's deliverance of and provision for Israel. The people sang them as they walked, those Psalms were road songs, freedom songs for the journey.

In the middle of Jerusalem stood the temple of God where heaven and earth touched in the Most Holy Place. Psalms of ascents were not only about going to the feasts in Jerusalem but about coming into the temple and presence of God. Psalm 130 is especially appropriate for ascending toward the throne of God, because it images an upward rising from despair and sin.

Out of the depths I cry to you, O Lord;
O Lord, hear my voice.
Let your ears be attentive to my cry for mercy.
If you, O Lord, kept a record of sins,
O Lord who could stand?
But with you is forgiveness;
Therefore you are feared.
I wait for the Lord, my soul waits,

and in his word, I put my hope.
My soul waits for the Lord
more than watchmen wait for the morning,
more than watchmen wait for the morning.
O Israel, put your hope in the Lord,
for with the Lord is unfailing love
and with him is full redemption.
He himself will redeem Israel
from all their sins. (Psalm 130)

Christians have long used Psalm 130, as a penitential prayer, acknowledging sin and receiving the grace of forgiveness and ascending once more into the presence of the one true God.

Tabernacle and Temple imagery as the focal point of God's presence resolves in Jesus the Messiah. As High Priest and sacrificial lamb, he opens the way for us to enter intimacy with God, or intimacy with God, again. Jesus, our great High Priest, offered his own blood in atoning sacrifice once for all. (See Hebrews 8-10.) At the moment of his bloody death on the cross, the veil in the Temple walling off the Most Holy Place was torn from top to bottom (Matthew 27:51); opening the way to God's presence to all who believe.

The New Covenant Temple is the corporate church, but individual Christ-followers are also carriers of the Spirit (1 Corinthians 5:19; Ephesians 2:19-23). Rising from the depths, then, does not mean we need to somehow climb up to God's presence. God has not moved.

What changes is our awareness of his Presence when we sin, our shame puts what feels like distance between ourselves and God. To rise and re-enter is to acknowledge, like the Psalmist, where we are and who God is:

"If you, O Lord, kept a record of sins,
O Lord who could stand?
But with you is forgiveness;
Therefore you are feared."

Like Israel before us, who famously went astray, Christ-followers have spotty records. When we are low, we need to remember there is a way up. What do you do with your sin, guilt and shame? Do you rationalize, in some self-righteous rant, "Well at least I'm not as bad as that guy," or minimize it, "It's no big deal, everyone else is doing it." Do you claim victim status by blaming others or the "system" as a way to avoid calling sin by its true name? Or maybe you even conclude your sin not sin at all but an expression of freedom.

Psalm 130 reveals God's mechanism to deal with our transgressions. We can face them honestly; we do not need to play games of rationalization to mask them. Nor do we need to descend into self-hatred as people who have no hope.

The next time you find yourself making excuses for your sins or dumpster diving into self-loathing when you see them, remember God's unfailing love and forgiveness laid down in Psalm 130.

Likewise, the next time you are riding high, think of Psalm 130. Recall the journey up to God's presence, is to move together as did Israel. Fellow travelers in the depths need your encouragement and comfort. Look around you, find them, remind them of Psalm 130. (Swimming alone in the ocean or traveling solo to Zion is inadvisable on so many levels!)

Finally, whether we find ourselves high or low, the Psalm is a song of joy we sing together. If we sing it loud enough, folks not traveling with our caravan will hear. The open-hearted ones will listen to the gospel in the lyrics, join the march and take up the song all the way to Zion.

QUESTIONS FOR REFLECTION AND DISCUSSION:

1. Are you more likely to own and acknowledge your sins or do something else? Explain.

2. Is the God the Psalmist describes, the God in whom you believe? List the similarities and differences.

3. Put yourself in the place of the Psalmist, write down the feelings and thoughts you experience.

4. Have you thought of your church mates as fellow travelers? If you did, what difference would it make?

5. What other thoughts or questions did the reading stir in you?

JUDGMENT: PART 1

"**K**nowing what you don't know" is a valuable asset when considering other humans. A few years ago, I attended a Little League baseball game to watch my grandson play. These games are famously torturous for highly competitive parents (and grandparents) who forget how inept they were when they played Little League. Case in point: at 7, I attempted to steal second with the bases loaded.

I sat on a grassy hillside above the diamond with my wife. Just down the slope from us was a woman with three or four very active children buzzing around her like angry bees, pushing, fighting, and slurping on sugary frozen desserts. She paid little attention to the bees unless one flew too close—earning a sharp rebuke or a slap.

The woman, mid-thirties and heavily tattooed, sported a very revealing top, along with short-shorts, and I immediately had her pegged. Single mom, probably a drug user, on Welfare with kids from several different sperm donors. The kids were disheveled, undisciplined, probably unwanted and definitely out of control.

I'd never met the woman, mind you, but my judgments flashed without warning into my consciousness. I looked down the hill, and down my nose toward her, feeling smugly superior. I'd written her off as a human being.

The Holy Spirit not so subtly set my hypocrisy alarm off when I remembered the title of the message I was to deliver to our church that very weekend, "Jesus on Judging." I was doing the very thing I would tell our church not to do—the very thing Jesus said never to do. In an instant, I'd made a judgment on the worth of a person I did not know based solely on outward appearances. I was a hypocrite (actor wearing a false face), because I was playing the part of God.

The game, being what it was, I had time to reflect and repent of my self-righteous attitude. I asked for God's forgiveness and thought about from where my automatic judgmentalism arose. One answer came to mind quickly, the woman's rough and suggestive exterior, the unruly kids, fit a "profile" stored away in my mind—"Oh, she's one of those people."

Sure, prejudgment can be accurate. If a man is wearing a Swastika and shouting Nazi slogans, one does not need to assume much to believe he leans toward a particular worldview. But the lady I was judging had no such blatant advertisements attached. Ignorant prejudice tends to fill in the blanks when we lack real information.

In essence, I'd sinned grievously against the woman, writing her off as an inferior specimen of humanity. No wonder Jesus warned us not to judge. I had placed her "beyond the pale"—a saying derived from ancient times when undesirables were exiled outside the last vestiges of light from the campfire, the center of warmth and community fellowship. Putting people "beyond the pale" is the judgment of condemnation and, again, way above my pay grade.

Such judgment is the heart of evils like racial prejudice, and when fully grown and expressed, often turns violent tearing at the fabric of societies. The recipients of our judgments are usually those who look or believe differently than us, and for most of us, the judgmental attitudes are so baked in, they escape our notice. Scripture reminds us that superficial judging also goes on in the church of all places (James 2:1-4).

But God did not let me put the woman surrounded by the buzzing bees "beyond the pale." God thankfully stopped me in the very act.

My first impulse was to apologize, but that would have made things much worse. Where would I begin? "Oh, I just wanted to say I'm sorry for thinking you were a loose unfit mom." (I did not even know if the kids were hers!) Or maybe I could start a conversation about her tats? Uh, no, too much like a come-on from an old man.

Here is what I did do. I began by using myself as an example of the sort of judgment Jesus prohibits by telling the story of my inner dialogue at the ballpark in all its disgraceful detail as part of my message that weekend.

I spent time reflecting on the reason Jesus told us never to pretend we were God and judge others. God is the only one with all the information. I also remembered that even if my judgment of the woman was correct, I had no authority to "write her off." God had not written her off. God loved her as much as he loved me and either had or was seeking a relationship with her.

Now, by God's grace and with varying degrees of success, I try to correct my flash judgments—especially of people I don't know, which is only a start. I could say more, of course, about my critical opinions of those I do happen to know, but that would take more public repentance and another reading.

QUESTIONS FOR REFLECTION AND DISCUSSION:

1. If God judged you like you judge others (Matthew 7:2), how would you be judged?

2. Are you aware of "baked in" profiles (prejudgments) of specific people or even people groups with whom you are not personally familiar? Name them.

3. Why is it essential for us to become aware of our tendencies to prejudge others?

4. What other thoughts or questions did the reading stir in you?

JUDGMENT: PART 2

"**S**top judging me!" The teen, caught in bed with her boyfriend, shouted at her mother. In our society "judging" has become just about one of the worst things a person can do. Jesus himself is invoked to make the case, sometimes by people who seem to value little else he had to say. "Do not judge, or you too will be judged" (Matthew 7:1). But, what did he mean? Indeed, the recoil of the judgment of God is in view for those who judge, but is there anything Christ-followers can say about human behavior they deem wrong or destructive without violating Christ's command? Is it possible to disagree with a person's behavior on religious and moral grounds while still loving the person? It must be, my parents did so for years!

But, today, ocean swimmers (Christ-followers) are frequently called judgmental by those with whom we have moral disagreements. But, do not miss the irony. The charge of judging can itself be a judgment. If the culture police catch a Christ-follower 'judging,' they are quickly marginalized and condemned (judged). None of this is to say Christ-followers cannot become self-righteous judges! Of course, we can, and we too often do. (See Judgment: Part 1.)

Undoubtedly, moral relativism in our society has muddied the waters on what is considered right and wrong. Rabbi Jonathan Sacks tells us this is a profound and unwelcomed change.

> "Almost any condemnation of any private behavior {is being} dismissed as judgmental possibly for the first time in history in which judgment— usually seen as a virtue akin to wisdom has been regarded as a vice." (Jonathan Sacks, "The Great Partnership" p 148)[1]

Rabbi Sacks uses the English word "judgment" in the sense of discerning between right and wrong. Did Jesus prohibit such discernment? Is Jesus telling us never to make a judgment call on any behavior? Is it not okay for the mom in our opening story to declare her daughter's tryst immoral or wrong?

In Matthew 7:1 Jesus uses the Greek word "krino," which essentially means: "to Separate, make a distinction between, exercise judgment upon..." and can be understood depending on the context in which it appears in at least three ways.

1. Judicial judgment: As in a court of law.

2. Discerning judgment: As when an umpire calls balls and strikes or in moral/ ethical judgments, as when one determines right and wrong based on agreed-upon standards of conduct.

3. Condemning judgment: In short, this sort of judgment is God's purview. Ultimately, it is judging another person worthy of hellfire or more generally writing them off, determining to shun them or placing them "beyond the pale."

Jesus' teaching does not rule out the mother's judgment of her daughter's actions. It prohibits "writing her off" or condemning her. There is a difference (see Judgement Part 1). In the same passage where Jesus says, "don't judge" (Matthew 7:1), he also tells his disciples, "Do not give dogs what is sacred; do not throw your pearls to pigs"(Matthew 7:6). To make such a determination, a disciple must exercise the kind of judgment Rabbi Sacks laments is increasingly seen as a vice in our society.

Condemning judgment is ruled out for any human being chiefly because only God has all the necessary information to make such a determination. Ocean swimmers must not take the place of God, deciding who is damned or who is not. Ocean swimmers love all people, even those who mean to hurt us (Matthew 5:43-48).

"Discerning judgment" affirms a morality rooted in the character of God, the "higher source" of our moral/ethical pronouncements. Thus, sexually immoral behavior like the teen and her boyfriend engaged in can be judged wrong, especially by her mom. Mom does not need to condemn her errant offspring to judge her behavior as wrong. Nor do ocean swimmers need to shrink from affirming a morality that flows from God in the face of those who call us "judgmental."

None of the above requires us to become a "loud" moral police force, finding fault with everyone who breaks God's moral law! This approach loses on two counts: first, we often fall short of God's standard too! Secondly, correcting another human works best in the context of a mutual relationship (as in mother/daughter or the sibling bond in the church). Paul, writing to the Corinthian church even goes so far as to ask, "What business is it of mine to judge those outside the church" (1 Corinthians 5:12a)? Finally, both Jesus and Paul teach in Matthew 7:3-5 and Galatians 6:1-2 respectively, correction of others in the family must be done with great caution, asking God for a keen sense of our own sinfulness, a profoundly loving humility and a desire to build up and not tear down.

Does this mean we abandon taking a moral stand against the evil behavior we witness in the world, outside the church? No, it does not. Evil must be called out based upon the higher authority of the character of God never forgetting we, too, are judged by the same rule. Then, we proceed fearlessly but cautiously, combating injustice, sexual immorality, greed, hateful behavior, religious bigotry, and a host of other evils.

We are to prophetically "speak the truth in love" in public discourse and not be silent; never in self-righteous condemning terms but as the embedded preservers of salt and the loving illuminators of light (Matthew 5:13-15).

Swimming in the ocean requires judgment calls. Holding one's course in today's relativistic tides and currents call for a skillful navigator. The Navigator is God who reveals his laws and judgments in scripture illumined by the Holy Spirit. Be humble, not silent.

QUESTIONS FOR REFLECTION AND DISCUSSION:

1. Have you ever been called judgmental? Was the charge accurate considering the above reading?

2. Why is a relationship so significant when bringing correction?

3. Why does Jesus command self-inspection before going to correct a brother or sister?

4. How should a Christ-follower speak into a culture at odds with his or her higher moral authority?

5. What other thoughts or questions did the reading stir in you?

END NOTES:

1. Sacks, Jonathan. The Great Partnership. Schocken. 2011

THE MAN

Read Genesis 24

"Sometimes I drown under the burden of insignificance as if being somebody was everything. Better to forget oneself while doing good." – Unknown.

The Patriarch Abraham, the keeper of the "promise," and his wife Sarah had a 'miracle baby' whom they named Isaac (which means something like laughter); thus named because 100-year-old Abraham's 90-year-old wife became pregnant, with Laughter (Isaac). Everyone was laughing, not least ancient Abraham and Sarah. Isaac would become the carrier of the promise God gave Abraham: his offspring would one day bless the entire planet.

There was a problem. After Laughter grew up, where would the elderly Abraham get him a wife so that he could produce offspring? Canaan, where they lived was ruled out, offering a bride-pool full of idol worshipers. Something had to be done, and it is here "the man" appears on the scene.

He was Abraham's man, his most trusted associate (Genesis 24:2)—someone he could rely on to perform a vital mission, securing a bride for Isaac. The bloodline of the promise was at stake, but "the chief servant" upon whom Abraham, the "father of faith," would rely is never named; identified in the story only as the 'chief servant,' 'servant' or, "the man."

Some would say it is not crucial in the inspired author's purpose to name the chief servant. He was a necessary role player in the larger story of how God shaped the Messianic line. Duly noted, but the servant's anonymity reveals another point that ocean swimmers must absorb, because most of us, too, will be nameless in the great story of God.

So, what can we learn from the nameless man in Genesis 24? First, that he is a gifted man who, over time developed his talents. That is, he had risen to his position of authority in Abraham's household by improving and demonstrating his skill set. The skills included leadership (the chief servant ran the family), business acumen, decisiveness and the requisite knowledge of Ancient Near Eastern etiquette. He was a skilled negotiator fit for representing a man of means. The lesson for us is clear: do the best you can with what you have.

A high character also shows up large in "the man," not least, the traits of loyalty and faithfulness. "Character" is not the same as talent or giftedness. It emerges from deep-seated principles.

Genesis 24 recounts how the servant stayed doggedly "on mission" with a pointed single-mindedness. He focuses on his task by avoiding the pleas of the crafty Laban, brother of Rebekah, Isaac's future wife. Laban wants to delay the mission probably to extract more gifts from "the man's" wealthy master.

Abraham's trust in the "servant" flows not only from the man's talent but also his well-developed character qualities. This combination always opens the door to more responsibilities and opportunities to serve.

What about the servant's faith in God? That is a little harder to trace from the story. A few lines of thought are possible. In the Ancient Near East, Abraham's view of "one creator God" was rare if present at all; not unlike what is increasingly detectable in the Postmodern Western world, where there are gods galore to worship. But the servant has respect and even awe for what he calls the "God of his master Abraham."

As the story unfolds, this "faith" seems to grow as his mission moves from one stage to the next. We see him throwing up a desperation prayer to "his master's God" upon arriving at a well where Rebekah (Isaac's future wife) is present to draw water. When God grants, in exquisite detail, precisely what the servant prayed for a moment before the actual events unfolded, "the man" takes a giant step toward his master's God.

Another way to understand the faith of the servant is to see it as already formed under the influence of the Patriarch. When he refers to Yahweh as his "master's God," it may merely be a sign of respect toward Abraham and God. Whether the servant came to faith during the mission or he merely grew more deeply in his trust of the God of Abraham, makes no difference. The point for me is that carrying out God's mission always matures and deepens faith.

For ocean swimmers—who will mostly remain nameless—loyalty to the master's calling, developing the gifts and talents God gives; then, persistently carrying out the mission itself, forms the operational framework for being a faithful and effective servant.

This framework is how single mothers take a less prestigious job to be there for their children as they grow through their formative years. It is how a dad turns down a career move in favor of leaving his family in one place to maximize their development. It is how a pastor faithfully labors in an inner-city ghetto without seeing the usual trappings of what is called success. It's fidelity to one's assigned task, whatever it might be that God blesses. The nameless servant of Abraham was nothing if not faithful.

Sadly, this is not the framework of the world in which we live. Our culture's context is all about maximizing one's options rather than faithfulness or loyalty and almost demands the seeking of recognition. Earning money, having good looks, sexual prowess, and winning are classic ways we use to measure our worth. Absent these things, we turn to social media to advance our "brand." Fear of being an unknown in our culture is seemingly too much to bear and, some in extreme cases, even resort to mass murder to become "somebody."

Don't misunderstand feeling good about ourselves as God's image bearers and God's children define a healthy sense of "self" based on telling ourselves the truth about who we are and rejecting demonic lies and slander that undermine our God-given identity. But this is not the same as seeking to "make a name for ourselves" as did those who built the Tower of Babel (Genesis 11:1-9). The difference is the tower builders tried to become significant apart from God.

Bottom line: if God wants your name to be known, that's fine. He will make it known and if you find yourself a celebrity, make the most of the opportunity to serve God. But until God brings you to such a place, just do your job. Along the way, be like the "man" continuing to hone your skill set in preparation for any task to which the Master might call you.

Finally, like Abraham's servant when we faithfully follow God's purposes, we will find ourselves coming to know God better. More and more, God will become "our God." Similarly, our unwavering focus on the tasks God assigns will usher in the miraculous invasion of God's kingdom. Note, again the fine-tuned, detailed prophecy God used to aid "the man." (Genesis 24:41-49) God's power accompanies faithful obedience to the assignments he gives us (Mark 16:15-20).

When I am content to be "completely unknown" like Abraham's servant, I am free from the distraction of making a name for myself, worrying about what others think of me and stressing over "making things happen." As is so often said by so many, it's not about us anyway. The story is about God and his kingdom, and it is our privilege to play a part.

Remember, above all, God knows your name, and when you hear God call your name at the end of all things, you will rise to meet him. That's the real pay-off, friends, dwarfing recognition in this current evil age.

QUESTIONS FOR REFLECTION AND DISCUSSION:

1. When it comes to the mission(s) God has called you to perform, how are you like the "man" in Genesis 24? How are you unlike him?

2. How has our recognition-seeking culture shaped the way you serve God?

    a. Not at all

    b. Moderately

    c. Massively so

    d. Other

3. What would you change about how you serve others if you were content with receiving no recognition?

4. Are you developing your gifts and talents for the mission God has called you to do? How?

5. What does it mean to you that God knows your name?

6. What other thoughts or questions did the reading stir in you?

LOSS

Ocean swimming always involves loss. We lost Kate at eighteen months, and the following is my journal entry which became a reading at Kate's memorial. Nothing profound here besides the tragedy itself. I place the text here in the hope it may comfort other swimmers who find themselves in the midst of loss.

> Still, now her dancing feet. Kate went to live with Jesus today and in my heart is a rage at the prince of death that explodes from my throat in a useless scream. So pale and tender is she, taken away from loving parents, doting sisters, unborn brother. And, I ask the Lord, "Why, raise Jairus' little girl and not Kate?" (Mark 5:21-24, 35-43)

But "why" is a pointless query in the face of senseless, unspeakable loss. The relevant questions are WHERE, WHEN and WHAT. What are you saying, Lord Jesus? What shall I do now? Where's my child? Where are you? Will I see her again? These questions have answers.

Answers to the "where" questions are close at hand: Kate is with God, in Christ. She is with others lost to us, some even before they were born. Where is God? God is with those who trust him even when they don't see him. We know all of this because God proved his love and faithfulness in the life, death, and resurrection of Jesus the Christ. He has conquered death, and his love never fails.

The "what" questions are harder to trace. What is Jesus calling parents ravaged by the worst this fallen world can dish out to do? Certainly, honor the life and the memory of Kate, always. Let her be spoken of and cherished, let the pictures and videos be seen and not banished for fear of pain. Celebrate her life, every moment of it! You will need those memories to keep your love warm until you meet her again in the arms of Jesus.

Another answer to "what" lives in the womb of Kate's pregnant mom. Still, more answers are seen in Kate's siblings who will fill the house with laughter and tears. In fact, so much "what" is coming that life will catch you up again in its joy, love, pain, and adventure. "What now, Lord"? The answers continue to grow in ways beyond anyone's guess.

But for those of us who long to meet Kate again, the burning question is "when"? Surely, we are not called to "play God" by manipulating or hastening our "personal when." But for each of us "when" will come.

If we want to find Kate and the others, we will decide to follow the "narrow way" until we hear a voice calling us through an open door.

It is the voice of Jesus, and if you hear it and recognize it, you'll walk right into a family reunion beyond your wildest dreams. And when you see his face, some questions just won't matter anymore.

QUESTIONS FOR REFLECTION AND DISCUSSION:

1. Do you agree or disagree with the statement in the reading above? "Why is a pointless query in the face of senseless, unspeakable loss." Explain.

2. Faith in God is the key thread of the reading with respect to dealing with loss. How might the why, what, where, and when questions be dealt with apart from God?

3. What sort of questions will "not matter anymore" when we see the face of Jesus?

4. What other thoughts or questions did the reading stir in you?

BEHOLD THE MAN

*Read John 19:1-6, Genesis 1:26-28; 2 Corinthians
5:21; 2 Corinthians 3:18.*

J esus was everyman, standing there beaten up,
bleeding, ruined by sin. By contrast, the royal
robe and rude crown of thorns in mock fashion
mark God's real purpose for humans—vice-regents, in
God's image.

How sin has ravaged that image! What a picture of
fallen humanity. No wonder when we see him thus, we
turn away, repulsed. Because when we look upon his
brokenness, we see our own.

Even Church-going religious people turn away from
the battered Christ, putting up with facsimiles–haloed
icons, pale Galileans, which are not Christs at all. Mel
Gibson's Christ is closer to the truth, and who can look
at him for too long without seeing themselves?

As Pilate said, "Behold the man," God bids us look
deeply into the person we are, and remember Christ
absorbed our ugliness and sin until he becomes,
himself, the very things from which we turn away in
shame (2 Corinthians 5:21).

Proper gratitude and worship for the restoration of
our original faces (as God's image bearers) can only

reach the most poignant celebration as we learn to "behold the man." As I am willing to gaze upon the battered Christ, I come to grips with who I was, how wondrous God's willingness to restore me is, and the giddy hopefulness of complete restoration.

QUESTIONS FOR REFLECTION AND DISCUSSION:

1. What best describes your approach to Good Friday?

   a. Get it over with because Sunday's coming!

   b. I try not to dwell on the bloody sacrifice part of the gospel.

   c. I feel guilty, but don't exactly know why.

   d. Other

2. Has the church sanitized the suffering Christ? How and why?

3. Might gazing upon the battered Christ realign the way you worship on Easter weekend? If so, how?

4. What other thoughts or questions did the reading stir in you?

READING 44

TICK TOCK

On my 55th birthday, I sat in my workspace looking at my books and feeling satisfaction in how many I'd read. And then, suddenly (and I'd never noticed this before), I heard the ticking of the clocks. They were insistent and loud, one in front on the bookshelves and one in back plastered to the bulletin board. They seemed to me like the voice of God saying, "Make the most of your time in these evil days." They reminded me of my mortality and all that's left to do. Tick tock, Tick, tock... I may never be able to ignore them again; I might need to acquire silent clocks so I can go back to sleep. These were rude messengers, especially on one's birthday.

After healing a man blind from birth, Jesus told his associates: "As long as it is day, we must do the work of him who sent me. Night is coming when no one can work. While I am in the world, I am the light of the world" (John 9:4,5).

Just as I became aware of the ticking clocks on my birthday all those years ago, Jesus' words above remind me that the church is now "the light of the world"(Matthew 5:14) and there is a lot left to do. Question is: Am I doing it?

Guilt is an inferior motive, but if it stimulates action, it's better than doing nothing. God will sort out our motives on the way! The work is urgent since tomorrow is not a guarantee to any of us.

What is the work? In the context of Jesus' statement above, it is announcing good news to a lost world—every ocean swimmer's assignment. We declare it intentionally by deeds and words, always conscious of every opportunity that God brings our way (Ephesians 5:18).

The assignment goes beyond the conventional idea in Evangelical circles called "witnessing," which implies using persuasive words to win people to Christ. But "witnessing" and being "witnesses" are not the same thing. A witness speaks when needed, but the gospel shows up, perhaps most vividly, in how I live my life. Putting it succinctly, I must be the good news, intentionally.

Tick Tock is not only about God's mission through me, but in me. I can "good news" with word and deed until I'm blue in the face, but if I am testy and unloving it becomes like a noisy, irritating guitar riff that hurts peoples' ears. If Jesus is not Lord in my attitudes and emotions, if I'm not pushing on towards Christ-likeness as did Paul (Philippians 3:12-16) but, instead, settle in my selfishness, bad temper and lack of self-control, I blur the message beyond recognition.

The clocks awaken me—persistently warn me, that being like Jesus is still a long way up the road and things must change inside, because night is coming when no one can work.

Finally, pictures of my children and grandchildren lining the shelves and walls of my office remind me of the investment God calls me to make in those he gives me to love. Tick Tock and they're grown, no longer accessible to my influence or merely gone ahead into the next life. Does my calendar include time with them?

The ticking machines that interrupted my birthday slumber proffer a soft alarm to help me stay awake and in the game until the dawn comes and daylight never ends.

QUESTIONS FOR REFLECTION AND DISCUSSION:

1. In what ways has God alerted you to how you are using time? Explain.

2. God and his mission, becoming like Jesus, and loving family and friends are priorities the Bible urges upon us. What are the primary time thieves that keep you from these things? Make a list.

3. Read Ephesians 5:15-17. What is the central message you hear from this text? Explain.

4. What percentage of your time is devoted to the priorities mentioned in question two, above?

5. What other thoughts or questions did the reading stir in you?

CARDINAL

The male cardinal is attacking my window kamikaze style. His claws cling to the window screen, then body and feathers bump against the glass of my air-conditioned office. He is frantic, like he wants to bring me an urgent message but can't penetrate. Maybe he wants to tell me about something in his world. Perhaps he is trying to get away from something pursuing him, and my office looks like shelter. Or just maybe he's been sent by God to warn me about how people like me who live in artificial worlds are ruining his. His redness reminds me his errand is desperate, like blood spurting from a severed artery. The scarlet feathers also suggest the priestly nature of his visit—a bridge between my world and his.

Should ocean swimmers care about the physical world? Should Christ-followers be environmentalists? Some, as a pastor I was visiting with many years ago, would say, "Our priority is saving souls and teaching the Word of God." I was there soliciting his church's support for a seminar on environmental responsibility our church was conducting so I asked, "Doesn't the Word of God teach us it's a priority to obey the Cultural Mandate?"

When my question drew a blank, I went on, "The 'Cultural Mandate' is laid out in Genesis 1, (and other places) assigning responsibility to humans to take care of the planet. I then pointed out that as far as I knew, God did not rescind that Mandate. Our interview came to a rather abrupt end after that, as my tone was, perhaps a bit too sharp? Oh, well. The Mandate goes like this:

> "Then God said, 'Let us make man in our image, in our likeness, and let them rule over the fish of the sea and the birds of the air, over the livestock, over all the earth, and over all the creatures that move along the ground. So God created man in his own image, in the image of God he created him; male and female he created them. (Genesis 1:26-27)

Our assignment, as God's image bearers, is about dominion (not domination) of the world. We are to take care of things, make things livable for every creature God created (Genesis 2:15). So, yes, ocean swimmers must be environmentalists. But what about saving souls? Isn't that, as my colleague pointed out, our primary mandate? It is, but the Evangelical Mandate (aka "The Great Commission" Genesis 12:1-3; Matthew 28:18-20) does not cancel the Cultural Mandate; both are gathered up into God's plan to save the entire world (not just 'souls').

The Genesis author mentions God's assessment of his creative work as "good" no less than seven times in just the first chapter! Subsequently, God does not plan to destroy his "good" creation, as some have misconstrued a poor translation of 1 Peter 3:10 to teach. God intends to redeem his creation which, according to

Romans 8:22, is "groaning" in futility until the "New Humanity" is revealed at the final resurrection.

Our restoration, then, is tied tightly to the culmination of God's project, the New Heaven and the New Earth.

> Then I saw a new heaven and a new earth, for the first heaven and the first earth had passed away, and there was no longer any sea. I saw the Holy City the New Jerusalem, coming down from God, prepared as a bride beautifully dressed for her husband. And I heard a loud voice from the throne saying, "Now the dwelling of God is with men…" (Revelation 21:1-4)

The scene in the text above is a marriage God always intended between himself and his people in a New Creation. Here is a sprinkling of passages that affirm the marriage motif: Isaiah 54:5, 62:4-5; John 3:29; Ephesians 5:31-32. But, remember, the joining together is not merely between God and his people, but heaven and earth. It is a coming together of the physical creation and the spiritual creation; God's seen and unseen world. Jesus' resurrection body preceded and modeled what was to come. Physicality and spirituality joined are our future.

All of the above means ocean swimmers do well to honor and preserve our physical environment as we honor and protect our physical bodies in anticipation of the glorious transformation of both. In short, we value what God values.

Because we love people and God's creation so much, we don't treat the earth like some people treat a rental car. What sort of planet are we leaving those who come after us and what, after all, is "Christian" about trashing or neglecting our common home? The priority of love alone charges ocean swimmers to take care of the planet.

Because our physical oceans are becoming more and more degraded, the theme of these devotions, namely "swimming in the ocean," becomes more than a metaphor for living an engaged, fruitful life. (See Reading 1) One example of the deterioration of our oceans is "dead zones"(hypoxia zones).

Dead zones are areas (in some cases hundreds or thousands of square miles) where oxygen has been depleted from the water due to agricultural wastes that run off the land into rivers, streams, and end up in our oceans. The results include, but are not limited to, massive fish kills and the destruction of other sea life.

A second severe issue in the oceans surrounding Earth's continents as well as our rivers and streams is the epidemic of "plastic pollution." Thousands of metric tons of plastic find their way into these bodies of water every year. A scientist friend told me he estimates there are more pieces of plastic in the ocean than fish!

Biologicaldiversity.org puts it this way:

> "We're surrounded by plastic. It's in the single-use packaging we discard, the consumer goods that fill our stores, and in our clothing, which sheds micro-plastic fibers in the wash. In the first decade of this century, we made more plastic than all the plastic in history up to the year 2000. And every year, billions of pounds of plastic end up in the world's oceans."[1]

One of the many results of plastic pollution in the ocean is the adverse effect on the life forms God created to inhabit them. For example, Albatross mothers often feed their young plastic pieces mistaking them for food. The chicks' bellies fill with plastic over time, and they end up starving (it is awful to see). Other animals ingest the plastic as well. There are many more examples of environmental toxicities humans have had a hand in unleashing into the world, but these make the point, I think.

To our disappointment, the conference I was pitching to my pastor friend all those years ago met with indifference in our area churches and, in subsequent years, I've noted little change. So, my "ask" to you dear reader is to allow this devotion to be for you a message from God like the cardinal urgently attacking my window was for me. The news is: of all the people on Earth, Christ-followers, charged by God to be caretakers of the planet should be vitally aware of and involved with remedying problems that threaten our shared home.

Thankfully, the highly qualified speakers at our church conference gave those of us who attended practical ways to participate in preserving and caring for our little piece of God's good creation. In closing, I want to pass some of them on to you.

- Educate yourself on local and worldwide environmental issues. (Do your best to avoid political extremes as you do your research.)
- Vote for candidates who propose reasonable ecological protections.
- Check the "whys" on each of the following suggestions.
- Recycle.

- Curb your use of plastics—eliminating your use of disposable plastic water bottles could be a start.
- Join a group who plants trees in blighted areas.
- Join a group (maybe one your church starts) to clean up the litter around waterways in your community.
- Buy local whenever possible.
- Limit your use of fossil fuels.
- Only upgrade electronics when needed.
- Eat less meat. (This is one of the biggest practical actions people can take; it makes a big impact.)
- Only use fertilizer, pesticides, and herbicides when necessary.
- Plant native plants/remove non-native plants.
- Buy fair trade/organic.

QUESTIONS FOR REFLECTIONS AND DISCUSSION:

1. What has formed your opinions about caring for the environment most?

   a. News coverage

   b. My political party

   c. My faith

   d. Other

2. Does the idea that God cares about his physical creation alter the way you view the environment? If so, explain.

3. The cardinal flying up against my office window seemed to me like a message from God. What

"environmental care message" might God be trying to get through to you at this time?

4. Which of the above suggestions for doing earth-care appeal to you? What action steps might you take?

5. What other thoughts or questions did the reading stir in you?

END NOTES:

1. Center for Biological Diversity. *Ocean Plastics Pollution.* https://www.biologicaldiversity.org/campaigns/ocean_p lastics/

FORGETFUL GOD?

*"For I will forgive their wickedness and will remember
their sins no more" Jeremiah 31:34.*

That the omniscient God chooses not to
remember is a fascinating concept,
notwithstanding the chance Jeremiah may be
using God's "memory" as poetic imagery to say, God
doesn't "actually" forget, but will not hold sins against
us as if he remembered. That is possible, but other
Biblical texts seem to point to God's intentional, literal
forgetfulness (Psalm 103:11-12. Hebrews 8:12).

My take is Jeremiah's prophecy above gives a
glimpse of God's inner life, especially God's emotions.
Some would say God doesn't feel emotional pain and
suffering as we do, a characteristic of God known as
"impassibility." But impassibility is a Greek
philosophical idea that found its way into our theology.
I don't buy it. God seems to wear his feelings on his
sleeve in the text above and many other places in
scripture. A God who feels resonates with us who bear
God's image since we in a limited and broken way
experience the same emotions.

God's last Word to us is the incarnation of Christ,
which clinches the argument against impassibility for

me. Jesus experienced emotions and suffered. There is no break between his humanity and his Godness. When we "see Jesus we see the Father" as he told Philip (John 14:8-10). Taking on board the idea that God feels and suffers in like manner to ourselves opens us to a more profound revelation of God's nature and, especially his love for us.

How does all this relate to God's forgetfulness? My theory is as follows: God's inner life is unfathomable, so God accommodates the communication of who He is in scripture to help finite beings relate to an infinite person. So, the inspired writers, especially in the Old Testament, invoke the closest and most vulnerable of all human connections to describe Israel's relationship with God, namely, marriage. Wayward Israel is a harlot; God is the offended spouse.

If you have ever experienced the profound emotional pain of betrayal caused by the person who should have loved you most, the forgetfulness of God makes perfect sense. Loving the perpetrator of such pain seems humanly impossible. By which I mean, such pain will always leave a mark. Even if reconciliation occurs, the wound of adultery is tender to the touch, decades later it can still modify how the injured party loves and trusts the one who hurt them.

But the prophet Jeremiah, speaking for God can puzzlingly, refer to "virgin Israel" after thirty chapters of denouncing her as a whore.

After accusing Israel of shattering the marriage vow through the blatant adultery of running after other gods, the prophet indicates a stunning restoration of the relationship. Israel is once again a virgin. What's going on here?

If God's love is infinite, God's suffering too is beyond our understanding. God experiences emotional pain of the most intimate kind at the hands of those he created, redeems and sustains; those who should love him most. God's love, then includes fierce intensity, and vulnerability like but not identical to our idea of romantic love or even parental love; yet, it is infinitely more profound than either. God's love, as presented in scripture is not "Spock-like," robotically expressing his nature. God's love and how he intends to share it with humans as presented in scripture strains the margins of what we can grasp, as David wrote, "Such knowledge is too wonderful for me" (Psalm 139:6).

The alternative interpretation; God does not actually forget but merely rises above our harlotry is valid, of course, and also speaks of a robust love to be celebrated. But in light of the above, could it be that God chooses to forget our infidelities to free himself to love us without reservation? I think it could be.

How would an omniscient God do such a thing? On the cross, God freed Himself to love us as if we never sinned at all; as if we have never broken faith with him. Isaiah tells us God does this not for us alone, but "for his own sake" (Isaiah 43:25). Losing the burden and pain of our adulteries is intentional on God's part so he can love us as he desires; uninhibited by the memory of the genuine pain we inflict upon Him. If I'm right, it means God does not delight in me "in spite" of my unfaithfulness; he merely decides to forget it.

Such love is not irresponsible denial on God's part; he once (and for all) DID remember. On the cross, God experiences and absorbs the sin of those who will trust him. The cross; an event in space/time gathers up all our sins past, present, and future. The cross is the merciful intervention of God once for all.

An interesting thought experiment along these lines would be to imagine Jesus reflecting upon the battle scars on his wrists, side, and feet and thinking, "I don't recollect the reason for these marks, but I do remember the joy I feel when I see them" (Hebrews 12:2). We, on the other hand, must never forget what the scars tell us about God's pathos and the price Christ paid to secure our freedom.

What about the final judgment? How can God judge me without revisiting my transgressions? Once again, I think the answer is the cross. God declares people forgiven and righteous in advance of the final judgment. The future invaded the present in Christ. God "remembered" at the cross once and for all.

Someone might say, if God chooses to forget, the not-yet-renewed thinking of his subjects might be: "Ok, then I can continue in my pet sins since God will not remember them anyway!" Such thinking betrays a profound misunderstanding of the cross and the grace of God.

God's forgetfulness is not intended to tempt us to more betrayal, but if I am right, to free God to love us in an uninhibited way. Those who use God's forgetfulness as a "get out of jail free card" have, perhaps never known God's grace, appreciated God's sacrifice, or been in a friendship with God at all. When, as Christ's Bride we sin intentionally, it is more like betraying a spouse than breaking a rule. When I think of my actions in this way it drives me to repentance.

When I choose to keep sinning, there are still consequences. For example, when I sin, I feel true moral guilt—which tends to make me isolate myself from God's loving friendship. I don't feel worthy to come into God's presence. When I am not under the influence of God's presence, my heart is no longer as tender toward others, and my human relationships deteriorate. In effect, I enter a downward spiral from which escape is difficult. God hates sin because it kills people he loves. It isolates us from God and each other.

But if God forgives and forgets what, then does a verse like the following mean? "If we confess our sins, he is faithful and just and will forgive us our sins and purify us from all unrighteousness" (1 John 1:9).

This text makes it sound like God doesn't forgive or forget until we confess, but in truth, confession is for us, not God. God has worked the sin issue out on the cross, once for all. Confession is not a work we do to receive forgiveness. The word in Greek for "confess" means something like "to agree with." We come to our senses and agree with God that our harlot-like behavior is, indeed, sinful. God lovingly cleanses our guilty consciences and, in effect, frees us to reopen the friendship we adulterated.

God's forgetfulness yields many life-altering lessons for ocean swimmers if we pay attention. First, sin is actually worse than swimming in the artificial chlorinated pool. (See Reading #1.) Second, God's love is such that he became vulnerable in Christ to the point of allowing his creations to hurt him. Third, God is a person, not robot-like and unemotional. His love is not unlike marital or parental love; it is warm, passionate and bursting with life. Fourth, the cross has freed God to pour out unhindered love upon us even though we still sin. Last, God provides a way for us to stay "engaged," even after we have played the whore through heartfelt confession of our sin.

God sings this love song over those who trust him: "I keep no record of wrongs" (1 Corinthians 13:5c).

QUESTIONS FOR REFLECTION AND DISCUSSION:

1. How is your concept of God different from the one put forth in the reading? Explain.

2. How would the way you relate to God change if you believed he refused to "hold a grudge against you"?

3. Scripture tells us to "forgive as we have been forgiven" (Colossians 3:13). Such forgiveness includes "forgetting." What is the biggest challenge in this formula? How can we meet it?

4. Based on the reading, write a letter to God expressing your feelings for him.

5. What other thoughts or questions did the reading stir in you?

Reading 47

Show and Tell

Even though we grew up in the Midwest, moving back home after five years in Los Angeles produced a mild culture shock for my wife and me. The experience was not a bad thing; the change reinvigorated our lives and reengaged us with our families. I met Bill through a pastor at the church we landed in some months after we moved back home. A bright campus minister at a local university, with a heart to raise up leaders, Bill agreed to "disciple me. During the next five years, he shaped my life by asking great questions, encouraging me when I was depressed, and speaking wisely, even prophetically.

Our mentoring relationship continued during the next five years but not in a way either of us would have chosen. Bill schooled me by showing me how an ocean swimmer holds onto Jesus and integrity during times of horrendous pain and loss.

I watched and prayed with my mentor as his marriage collapsed because of unfounded unjust accusations against him. I observed how the charges were leveraged to alienate him from his two young children, resulting in his decision to resign as the youth pastor of the most fruitful and vibrant teen ministry in the city.

Suddenly, with considerable trepidation, I became a go-to friend for the friend who was my teacher. Bill did not resist being cared for but allowed himself to be vulnerable in our friendship. In great humility, he let me lead; a leadership for which I often felt inadequate. His humility allowed Jesus to be his strength, and Jesus put him back into the game during those five years.

Our roles switched back to where they belonged when Bill began a new career as a financial advisor. He helped my wife and me plan our economic future with the care and integrity he always employed when dealing with people. Thanks to Bill's guidance, we retired in a financial position that frees us to volunteer our lives to Christ's cause without needing payment.

Bill continues to pastor people through his business and the church. He pioneered a much-needed service to divorced people—turning his pain into a full-blown ministry—touching thousands floundering from the trauma of divorce.

Sadly, more hardships awaited; lurking in Bill's bloodstream was Hepatitis C, contracted from a tainted blood transfusion given him during knee surgery in the 1970s. This disease was destroying Bill's liver. I knew he would press on, and he did without whining over "the hand he'd been dealt" or playing the "victim card." Quite the opposite. He doubled down on helping others and wisely orchestrated a prayer chain of good friends to cry out to God for his healing. God answered those prayers and preserved Bill's liver until the cure for Hep. C rolled around in the twenty-first century. Mentors don't merely talk; they live and by living, show us how it's done.

My friend is an excellent ocean swimmer, and that life naturally is not absent of God's blessings. For the ocean swimmer, the greatest thrill in life is giving ourselves away in sacrificial love to others, which is how all humanity is wired if they only knew it. Bill's estate planning work, his mentoring, his service on church boards and the fruitful Divorce and Beyond ministry he fathered give him sweet fulfillment and a legacy of grateful people left better for his care, coaching, and love.

But perhaps Bill would say his fondest blessing from God is his second family—a great wife, two super kids, and the restoration of a loving relationship with the son from his first marriage. The children all bear the stamp of being fathered by a good man; God has restored all the enemy tried to steal and more. The story of the great ocean swimmer Job comes to mind.

Recently, I attended a retirement party for Bill at his home. He invited about thirty close friends to celebrate. A few years ago, friends did a similar thing for me. My son planned time at the event for guests to share stories and memories about me. I was the star of the show and gratified if a little embarrassed by the kind sentiments expressed. Given all the man showed and taught me over the years, I should not have been surprised when Bill flipped the traditional script at his retirement celebration, but I was.

After dinner, he gathered us into his large rec-room, sat in front of us on a stool and announced that he wanted to spend time thanking each of us for how we shaped his life. Calling us by name, moving from person to person he specifically detailed why he appreciated each of us. We all experienced his warmth, gratitude, and good humor. The great reversal he pulled that night reminded me of something Jesus might do, and isn't that the point of ocean swimming, becoming like the master? Bill is well on his way.

When I grow up, I want to be like Bill. My humble advice to those committed to swimming in the ocean is to find people who will "show and tell" you how to be like Jesus. Search for such mentors and when you find them, hold them fast and in high regard because they will never abandon you. Finally, please be conscious that you, too, are someone's "show and tell" person. Ask the Lord Jesus to show you who they might be and pass the heritage God entrusted to you. You might be surprised how many people hunger for it.

QUESTIONS FOR REFLECTION AND DISCUSSION:

1. Which of Bill's character traits impressed you most? Why?

2. Who are, or have been, your most positive mentors? How did they help you?

3. What do you learn from Bill about how an ocean swimmer responds to the pain and hardship?

4. In light of Bill's story, reimagine your retirement party, what do you want your legacy to be?

5. Are you currently mentoring someone? What do you learn from Bill that might make your mentoring better?

6. Do you believe sacrificial love is the path to maximum personal fulfillment? Why or why not?

7. What other thoughts or questions did the reading stir in you?

COMMON PEOPLE

"God must have loved the common people because he made so many of them." – Abraham Lincoln[1]

Whether the sixteenth President said it or not, it seems accurate that most of us are rather average citizens. Geniuses or high capacity people are indeed a minor portion of humanity. When we consider Jesus' famous parable of the talents with this in mind, it throws a new twist in the lesson (Matthew 25:14-30).

The master in Jesus' parable gave three servants money to invest "according to their ability" (Matthew 25:15 b). The servant with the most "ability" received five talents, the second one two, the third servant received one talent. Each of the servants had an equal opportunity given their "ability." The master rewarded the first two servants who were productive with an identical benediction: "Well done good and faithful servant! You have been faithful with a few things; I will put you in charge of many things. Come and share your master's happiness" (Matthew 25:21).

The master's reward does not seem to be based upon the volume of product, but faithfulness. No one is asked to do more than they can but to be faithful to use what they have for the master. The third servant, who buried the talent the master gave, was rebuked rather severely.

Traditionally, the parable has been interpreted to focus on the individualized application that one must do the best one can with God's gifts and talents—summed up in the old phrase "use it or lose it"—but the scope of the parable goes beyond individual moral lessons. That the characters in parables can represent whole swaths of humanity, even nations, must not be lost.

For example, in the parables of the kingdom, Jesus is speaking to Israel as a people not merely giving moral lessons for individuals. Israel was created by God to be his vessel of revelation, to "be a blessing" to the entire world (Genesis 12:2). God entrusted them with the message, but they kept it to themselves.

On this view, the third servant who buried his master's money might correspond to Abraham's errant offspring. The "faithful servants" who invested the master's money and earned more are the "true Israel" Jesus is launching to get God's project to save the world back on track.

It is, of course, still true that the story is about faithfulness, not talent or even results. But the third servant got me thinking of Honest Abe's alleged quote mentioned above. If he was right about the prevalence of ordinary people (and he was), it is not hard to see how the third servant might correspond to the mass of humanity while the multitalented servants whose ability was greater are a rarer commodity in the population.

Concerning capacity or as Jesus has it, "ability," the third guy is most of us. It is also interesting that Jesus makes the one-talent associate the negative example in the story. Why is the low capacity guy the unfaithful one? Jesus usually turns the tables making heroes of the ones we would not expect such as the poor, foreigners, or other marginalized folks. But in the parable of the talents, Jesus' standard teaching is reversed.

In this light, the parable is particularly eye-opening for ordinary people to use what we have rather than bury it. One of the implications of this view is to see Jesus provoking the "majority" of his hearers, the ordinary people of Israel, and, of course, those among the masses who would hear this story in the future.

It is too easy for one-talent people to feel inadequate; to get lazy and let the elite do the "heavy lifting." Too many of us compare ourselves to two- and three-talent people and find ourselves wanting, without much to offer, so we offer nothing at all. A symptom of this reality in the current North American church is the prominence of the professional clergy (two- and three-talent people?) hired to do the actual work of the kingdom.

Allowing "highly gifted folks" to do the stuff we should be doing is to bury the talent God gives us. It insults the master who gave us the talent to use for his glory. The weight of such behavior comes through in the master's pronouncement over the servant who did not utilize what his boss had given him.

> "You wicked and lazy servant... Take the talent from him and give it to the one who has ten the talents. For everyone who has will be given more, and he will have an abundance. Whoever does not have, even what he has will be taken away from him. And throw that worthless servant outside, into the darkness, where there will be weeping and gnashing of teeth." (Matthew 25:26-30)

Admittedly, the same structure might apply to any unfaithful servant. No one should suppress the gifts and talents the Master gives to further his purpose in the world. But reminding ourselves that one-talent people are the majority certainly provides the parable with a new "twist." To mobilize them is to release a vast army into service. Jesus' dire warning of "use it or lose it" should be particularly poignant for one-talent folks like you and me.

I thank God for the multi-talented people whose charge is to be responsible stewards of what God entrusts to them, but, once again, they are in the minority; they cannot do it by themselves. It is those of us with one talent, who must pay particular attention to using what we have. In a classic reference to the common people Jesus says, "You are the salt of the earth…you are the light of the world" (Matthew 5:13-14).

J.R.R. Tolkien in his famous "Lord of the Rings" trilogy grasps the vital role of ordinary people in his characterization of Hobbits. Hobbits are small, unassuming creatures who play a necessary part in the history of Tolkien's fantasy world called Middle Earth, because they are faithful with the gifts and assignments that fell to them. Without Hobbits, the story takes an evil turn into darkness. Most ocean swimmers are like Hobbits. God urges us to use what he gives. Jesus' parable of the talents should be a bracing wake up call to the gravity of our purpose in the world.

QUESTIONS FOR REFLECTION AND DISCUSSION:

1. Do you see yourself as a one-, two- or three-talent person? Explain.

2. Why is the Master's rebuke so harsh in the parable of the talents?

3. Why is faithfulness so important to God?

4. If the Master came to settle accounts with you today, how would it go?

5. What other thoughts or questions did the reading stir in you?

END NOTES:

1. Tullai, Martin D. *So Abe Didn't Say It, but He Should Have. Who Said It?* The Baltimore Sun. August 30, 1992. https://baltimoresun.com/news/bs-xpm-1992-08-30-1992243042-story.html

CALLING

One's calling or vocation stems from a Latin term (vocare) coming from the root word vox, meaning "voice." The voice emanates from an outside source bidding us to some meaningful task to help the world. It was initially associated with a religious calling to the Priesthood or Clergy, but that narrows the idea too far. Callings from God extend beyond professional church work.

Scripture tells ocean swimmers to glorify God in all we do (1 Corinthians 10:31). But ocean swimmers are also called by God to specific, meaningful service. Some of our callings have a shelf life, but the most important ones are lifetime affairs—things God "wired us up" to pursue for his glory and the benefit of others. In an authentic sense, the voice that calls us creates, empowers, and releases "our voice."

The apostle Paul experienced his dramatic calling on the road to Damascus (Acts 9:1-18). Such unambiguous callings are still happening. My friend, Lance, who as a seminary graduate on the West coast heard a call to plant churches on the East coast via a vision of a flame burning through the map of Long Island, New York, at the precise point God wanted him to begin! He obeyed, went there, successfully planted a church and helped many others start congregations on the Eastern Seaboard. Granted, most ocean swimmers will not receive such crystal-clear callings from God, but to mix metaphors, God will establish our voice if we have ears to hear.

Sometimes we become aware of our callings on the fly, seemingly by accident: "Oh yes, I knew deep down I was to pursue helping the elderly during a visit to my great uncle at the senior living home." Or, like my friend, Brian, whom we had to coax into going to a low-income housing project to hand out groceries. He came away with the strong conviction that God called him to serve the poor, which he is still doing decades later. Or my friend, Chuck, a lifelong construction professional who on the way back from a project in the inner city heard: "Chuck why not use what you know to build things in Africa?" He's spent the last decade doing just that. God's callings are as varied as the people he calls covering a massive array of different voices from architects to zoo-keepers. All these voices are, once again, for God's glory and the benefit of others. Upon hearing the calling that creates our "voice," the proper response is obedience.

For me, the calling was teaching the Bible. It happened this way. After my conversion in Southern California, I found myself in love with Scripture; I couldn't get enough of it. My wife and I went to Bible studies every night taking notes and devouring the content. I'm not saying I understood it all, far from it, but I couldn't put the book down. I knew I had to tell others about Jesus from the beginning and loved learning about God from my Bible teachers. As I watched them, I found myself thinking, "I could do that. I want to do that." That seed of desire set the stage for what happened next.

In those early days of ocean swimming, I was working as a stereo salesman. My habit was to have breakfast near the place I worked on Ventura Boulevard in Studio City, California. Over coffee and a bran muffin, I read Scripture and wrote little commentaries on what I thought the text was saying in my journal. One morning, as I was practicing this ritual, I had an intersecting thought that stopped me dead still. "One day you'll be teaching this book." Emotionally, I went from neutral to tears and answered the voice, "There is nothing I'd rather do than teach this book." The encounter took me off guard but passed as quickly as it came. I paid my bill and walked out of the place wiping a tear from my eye and not a little puzzled by what had just happened.

Later that same day while at work, I received a phone call from the leader of our small Bible study group. "I need to tell you something that happened when I was praying this morning." He said. "Okay," I said, wondering about the urgency in his voice. "While I was praying, I think I heard the Lord say that you are supposed to take over facilitating our Bible study." Instantly my mind went to the weird encounter I had at the restaurant that morning. The two seemed connected, and while I felt deeply inadequate to teach a group in which most of the participants knew more about Scripture than me, I said, "I think it's the Lord," and quickly told him about my breakfast experience. With what might be called uneven results, I've now been teaching the Bible for the last forty years. It is my calling.

What is your calling? Until you discern, accept, and practice it, the voice God wants you to project for his glory will be muted. Your ocean swimming story will be incomplete, and more importantly, it hinders the story of God. I've always enjoyed the following take on discovering calling, and perhaps it will be helpful to you.

"The place God calls you to is the place where your deep gladness and the world's deep hunger meet." Frederick Buechner[1]

QUESTIONS FOR REFLECTION AND DISCUSSION:

1. If you know your calling, or "your voice," define it on a sheet of paper.

2. If you do not know you're calling, what is your best guess?

3. Are you acting out your calling? Why or Why not?

4. Why is receiving and acting on our callings so important to God?

5. Is Buechner's quote above helpful for you? In what way?

6. What other thoughts or questions did the reading stir in you?

END NOTES:

1. Buechner, Frederick. *Wishful Thinking: A Theological ABC*. Harper & Row. 1973

CHOOSING

My first and only attempt at skydiving powerfully illustrates that there are decisions in life from which there is no turning back. Once you leave the airplane, the die is cast, and you must live with all that comes next. You know this at the moment before you jump and in spades right after. Fateful decisions we take in life become known by the fruit they produce. If taken thoughtlessly or in the heat of passion, the consequences can be tragic. Equally making no choice, as the old saying goes, really is a choice and can be deadly. Asking the Father to make us aware of the choices we make each day in the light of his presence and wisdom is a good prayer. May we be wise enough to see the implications as clearly as I did when I jumped from a perfectly good airplane at 13,000 feet.

One standard but unwise decision-making method alluded to above might be called "analysis paralysis" producing no decision at all. Ocean swimmers need to know that analysis is fine but never as a cover for "fear of failure." Analysis paralysis occurs when we attempt the impossible task of removing all risk. But a life bereft of risky, no-turning-back decisions is not compatible with robust ocean swimming. Much of what

God calls us to do involves risk. John Wimber, the first national director of the Vineyard and one of my mentors, used to say faith is spelled "r-i-s-k."

That John practiced what he preached is borne out by his life and legacy. He made the sort of risky decisions ocean swimmers are called to make. Wimber was a successful musician with a potentially lucrative career ahead of him when he was apprehended by Christ, which changed everything. He loved to talk about being "a coin in God's pocket" to be spent in any way the Lord desired.

John's faith decision to lay down his music career and follow the Master's calling would positively impact thousands of other ocean swimmers to do the same, launching the Vineyard church planting movement. My wife and I attended one of the early meetings of the fledgling Vineyard experiment held in Palm Springs, California. We decided to jump out of the airplane, so to speak, and plant a Vineyard Church; that risk shaped the rest of our lives. Our church led hundreds of people to Christ over the years, and we were not the only ones who heard God's calling via John's challenge that day. Currently, there are about 1,500 Vineyard churches worldwide. Swimming in the ocean demands a life of risk-taking; the alternative is swimming in a sterile chlorinated pool. (See Reading 1.)

People take risks for different reasons. The risk of obeying God is entirely dissimilar to the motive of a real estate broker I met when I went jumping from the plane on that autumn afternoon. He did multiple jumps per weekend (sometimes as many as twenty). When I asked him why, he told me he was addicted to adrenaline. Jumping out of airplanes is what it took to remind him he was alive. Don't misunderstand, this form of recreation is neither evil nor wrong, just different from the risk-taking in which ocean swimmers are engaged. The real estate guy's reasons for risky behavior were about him; the chances ocean swimmers take generally concern God and His kingdom.

Another side of the decision-making spectrum includes choices springing from impulsive, unexamined passion; emotionally reacting to life's seemingly random events, inadvertently jumping out of airplanes we should never have boarded in the first place. Once again, such choices are more about the decider than God and His kingdom. Randy, an elder in the church we planted, had a safeguard against impulsive decisions. His rule was, "If I need to decide right now, the answer is no." This wisdom helped us avoid some silly choices.

One favorite Christ followers use when choosing impulsively is the time-worn, "God told me" excuse. Of course, God does speak to us today and sometimes calls us to do risky things. But when things go awry, and we come to see our decision was more about what we wanted than what God wanted, it's silly to blame God for the outcome. He gets blamed for everything that goes wrong already. None of this means God doesn't redeem bad choices for his glory; he does this all the time. What it means is ocean swimmers must learn to own the bad decisions we make and more importantly, to navigate between the extremes of analysis paralysis (a.k.a. fear of failure) and self-centered impulsiveness.

Since life consists of a series of choices, here are some questions for ocean swimmers to think about when making important decisions.

1. Is your decision consistent with God's word?

2. Is God speaking to you about your decision?

3. If married, is your spouse on board with your choices?

4. Are your close friends and church elders praying with you about this decision? What is their counsel?

5. Does taking this decision put others at risk or in danger?

Finally, returning to my sky-diving experience, I didn't risk the drop alone. No, I dove "in tandem" literally strapped to the chest of a sky-diving expert. The model for ocean swimmers is a lot like that; strap yourself to Jesus.

Enlist His counsel and the advice of his people Allow Him to shape the choices you make and be at peace with your decisions.

QUESTIONS FOR REFLECTION AND DISCUSSION:

1. In making decisions are you more like the analysis paralysis person above or the impulsive person? Explain.

2. How is God involved in your decision-making process?

3. Who are the closest counselors among your ocean swimming friends when making important choices? Can't think of any? Where could you find such counselors?

4. What risky decisions might God be challenging you to make right now? How is it going?

5. What other thoughts or questions did the reading stir in you?

CLOUDS WITHOUT RAIN

There is nothing worse than an apparently moisture filled cloud that brings no rain or a loud, thundering, lightning flashing front resulting in just a sprinkle. Sometimes we meet people who are like that, over-promising and under-delivering like the "man behind the curtain" who presented himself as the Great and Powerful Oz. Ocean swimmers must avoid phony presentations at all costs, because the hazards for those to whom we present Christ are perilous indeed.

Jesus said we would know false prophets by their fruit (Matthew 7:15). The fruit he refers to is debated but, at the very least, it includes self-aggrandizement using the Lord's name for personal gain. Watch out for lots of sparkle, glitz and personal promotion—all red flags indicating clouds without rain. Watch, too, that what you promise in Christ's name aligns with His leadership and His Word. Back in the 1970s, faith healers used to advertise their meetings with statements like; "come to watch blind eyes see and deaf ears hear." This is not a faith statement as much as it is an advertisement to draw a crowd and a better offering for the faith healer. God indeed may heal in spite of the self-promoter, but more likely, he or she is a cloud without rain having nothing to do with how God might move.

Ocean swimmers in the business community must also present their goods and services in ways that under-promise and over-deliver.

I once recommended a brother to remodel the house of a newly minted Christian friend who proceeded to delay her work, overcharge her, and demand payment when the work was not complete—capping off all of the above by not standing behind his job when it was found defective! He is a false advertiser, a noisy storm cloud without rain, a promise breaker. I cringed some decades ago when I saw his name in what was then called the "Christian yellow pages," a rag that advertised "Christian businesses one could trust." Perhaps he has changed, but the woman he victimized has struggled since with the promises of God because of the broken promises of the contractor.

The commitments we make to our families are perhaps the most important to keep. When we make promises to our kids regarding what we will do or never do again, we must take pains to follow through. Beware of making promises you can't keep out of guilt for past failures. Broken commitments or excuses are like clouds without rain passing over our spouses or children, leaving them distrustful and even with feelings of worthlessness. "I must not be worth much if he blows off his promise so easily," they reason. Admittedly, faulty reasoning but very common among the young.

God wants ocean swimmers to be clouds rich with rain, pouring showers of blessings out wherever we go. We don't need to stir up faith, pad our reputation, or assuage our guilt for past failures by announcing all the grand things we will do. Jesus said we should let our "yes be yes," and our "no be no." In sum: be generous in love, conservative with commitments, and boundless in our trust of the one who really brings the rain.

"For no matter how many promises God has made; they are "Yes" in Christ" (2 Corinthians 1:20).

QUESTIONS FOR REFLECTION AND DISCUSSION:

1. What are some of the reasons people over-promise and under-deliver?

2. Have you experienced broken promises from Christ followers? How did it affect your view of God and his promises?

3. What are some ways to avoid becoming a "cloud without rain" as described above?

4. What other thoughts or questions did the reading stir in you?

WHAT GOD JOINS TOGETHER

Forty-seven years ago, my remarkable wife and I were wed. Our honeymoon trip to a resort in French Lick, Indiana, (Yes, it's a real place in the world) might be seen as a metaphor for our entire life together; complete with thrills, strange twists, deep joy, mild tragedy, kind strangers, dumb fights, communication challenges, and much love.

On August 28, 1971, our wedding day, my bride (eighteen and innocent) and I a very green twenty-one, were embarking on a life together with scant preparation for what would face us. With the benefit of hindsight, I realize premarital training would have smoothed our journey, but alas we had none. **So, the first take away for those who plan to marry someday is: Get all the help you can beforehand, because you'll need it.** Excellent skills to hone are communication, budgeting, and understanding sexuality. These seem to be the most common areas of marital breakdown.

Everything at our wedding was mother-earth-ish, documenting the late hippy period in which our romance blossomed—and, thanks to my frugal mother-in-law, the wedding was very affordable. **Lesson number two: Married life is instantly made more stressful when elaborate and expensive nuptials leave all the planners and payers in physical and financial exhaustion.** Our wedding was great, and we had no post-ceremony economic blues. Financial blessing and restraint have marked our journey since, and I am grateful.

Keen to get the honeymoon started, we did not linger long at our late morning reception. We jumped into our Volkswagen bug, made a quick stop at her folk's house to grab our luggage, and set off for French Lick, some sixty-five miles south by way of narrow, winding country roads. The trip was longer and more eventful than we anticipated—twists, turns, and hills stopped us seeing what was ahead. One never knows what's coming around the bend in life. Best to be aware that "stuff happens," plan for what you can and trust God for the journey.

Lesson three: Expect the unexpected. Life, especially married life, is full of surprises some wonderful, some not. In forty-seven years, the shocks have been relatively mild, but they began on our honeymoon.

Well-wishers decorated the rear end of our VW Bug with multi-colored crepe paper streamers and the requisite "just married" signage on the windows all around. The streamers flying from the back louvers of the air-cooled engine would, a short time later, turn our well-meaning friends into unwitting saboteurs.

After driving about an hour, the heretofore trusty VW engine started to cough, and as we rose atop a high hill, she "gave up the ghost" on a narrow, lonely downgrade in Southern Indiana. It turns out, the air-cooled engine made a meal of the colorful crepe paper strips, sucking them into itself; she overheated. I tried to kick start the little Bug a few times rolling down the hill, but the engine would not turn over. We were marooned; this is how our marriage began.

Stress makes the ties that bind fray a bit, sometimes a lot. Many couples look to each other for help, but when neither knows what to do, the question "who's in charge" emerges. We knew we needed help but did not know from where in the steaming Indiana countryside it might come. As our dead car coasted down the long hill, we were about to find out.

At hill's bottom, on the right-hand side of the road, we saw a small asphalt parking area jutting back into the green foliage and noted what appeared to be a service station at the back of the lot. Our hearts quickened; was this an oasis? The sign on the concrete block building read: "Bardal's Bug Repair." Beyond all hope, our wounded Bug found its way to a VW repair shop in the middle of nowhere. What are the odds? **Lesson number four: In times of trouble, watch for a blessing.**

Marriages need uncanny blessings and unexpected friends along the way. Some folk might think, well, we never caught a break. But I bet, you did even if you didn't see it at the time. On our wedding day, we got a glimpse of "flash Providence." God loves people and loves marriage since he invented it (Genesis 2:20-25). Marriage without God can work, but why wouldn't we want the Almighty involved? Since then, there have been other interventions; some we know about, and no doubt, some we do not. We were not Christ-followers when we married—that came five years later after hurting each other so severely our marriage was on the verge of collapse, which is another painful story I won't recount here. But, on our wedding day, Jesus had his eye on us.

To our great disappointment, Bardal's Bug repair was closed on Saturdays. As a newly-minted husband, I answered the question above about who was in charge. My training in a patriarchal household dictated the man be in charge. The man should know what to do or at least pretend to know. So, I went up to the dingy, rusted metal front door of Bardal's concrete block building and banged away, hoping to raise someone. Mercifully, the boiling late afternoon August sunshine was waning—giving way to the relative coolness of the evening. My dear one climbed out of the unairconditioned Bug, leaned against the door and fanned her flushed face with a wedding program as I banged harder.

My wife saw him first, emerging from a house trailer parked on the side of the blacktop lot. "Can I help ya'll?" I turned from my knocking to behold a middle-aged man, clad only in boxers, sporting lily-white legs, and torso contrasting sharply with his brown neck and arms. He had what we used to call a "country tan." Limping badly from an earlier ankle sprain, obvious pain on his fat red face, ample belly welling over his boxers, he drawled, "Sorry 'bout your problem, but we's closed." My bride looked at him, then back at me. Her expression a weird combination of laughter with a hint of pure panic. This man was Bardal himself, the owner of the establishment.

"Car just quit," I said. "We rolled down the hill, saw your sign. I know you're closed but do you think you might take a look?" He nodded, half hopping over to the rear of the car. Opening the hatch, he tried to dislodge some of the burnt crepe paper from the seething engine; burned himself, cursed and spat out,

"She's overheated!" Wringing his hand in pain, he yelped, "What is that stuff?" (he did not say stuff).

"Well, we were just married up in West Lafayette," I stuttered, "and that sticky stuff is what's left of the crepe paper streamers our friends stuck to the back of the car. We were headed down to French Lick for our Honeymoon when the car died." "Well that was a dumb-ass thing for your friends to do," he said, angrily shaking his bullet-shaped burr-cut head. I nodded in emphatic agreement as if I knew my friends were indeed half-wits for pasting crepe paper on the back of an air-cooled motor. Trying to match his irritation, I blurted, "Those idiots! But what do we do now?" "Nothing to do but clean that crap (he did not say crap) off the engine when she cools—should be good to go after that." "How long?" I said, wanting to get the honeymoon show on the road as quickly as possible. "Mebbe an hour, I guess," he said, his tone softening considerably. Then with a sly smile on his broad face, Bardal gave us an invitation, "Why don't you honeymooners come into the trailer," pointing to his domicile on the far side of the asphalt lot. "She's airconditioned, and I got real cold beer!" How could we refuse?

Decked out in his checkered skivvies (he never put on his trousers), Bardal celebrated with us our new marriage in the best way he knew how. He provided us with a refreshing drink and a cool place to relax on a hot, humid summer day. He was hospitable even sharing his own honeymoon night with a story so colorful that I dare not repeat it here. He turned out to be a nice guy.

Lesson number five is this: Most people we meet along the way are pretty decent and favorable toward marriage; be open to their help. They usually want your marriage to work even if their own did not. Having a beer with Bardal taught us that people we would not generally befriend could become friends and not only in life's little crises. We have tried to return the favor Bardal showed us to other couples struggling with the unexpected twists and turns along the way of life.

The Bardal experience also yields a more general **lesson number six: Marriage needs allies.** Isolated unions assume the silly notion that our spouse is supposed to meet all our needs. That unrealistic expectation has shipwrecked many couples. We need family, friends, and the church to keep us accountable, healthy and worthy to live with our mates. God wants to provide all these things because again he loves marriage. Some of the friends God brings will be like Bardal—strange, awkward at first, but given a chance might prove the best friends of all.

After politely refusing Bardal's invitation to more beer and conversation, we finally pushed off to French Lick. The week there was romantic, awkward, fun, and not without some surprisingly epic disagreements. We were getting to know each other intimately, and for the record, as is the case with most inexperienced lovers, we were not very good at the sexual part of the arrangement. Truth be told we both felt like failures, having absorbed the romanticized myth that sex should always be amazing. It is not, but the good news is God's design for married sex develops over a lifetime, which happily means we get to practice until we get good at it. God's superb gift of sexual intimacy is just one of the many skills that need perfecting; more importantly, we have three outstanding adult children born of our union who have their own families now. God's plan when followed produces deep joy. **Lesson number seven is: Work on your sex life.**

Our first genuine fight was over a miniature golf game at French Lick. I lost the game and the fight. My young bride discovered I was a sore loser when I flung my putter after a miss. She was incredulous that I'd be so upset over losing what was to her a silly little game.

My mild tantrum revealed one of my numerous flaws, in this case, tying my very identity to winning or losing. My family was fiercely competitive, and I viewed my life somewhat like a sports stat sheet. Win you are good, lose you are, well, a loser. Secondly, defeat was made more intolerable in my mind by losing to a girl!

When I cooled off, I apologized to my bride but, in her eyes, the patina of my once noble character was smudged. **Lesson eight is: Marriage is a crucible that reveals flaws; acknowledging them allows us to cooperate with God as he transforms us into the people he wants us to be.** Conversely, without such awareness becoming God's best version of ourselves for his glory and our mate's blessing is hindered.

Forty-seven years of matrimony have pushed things to the surface in both of us that were not pretty. Marriage is one of the most effective atmospheres for spiritual growth. Stretching and sometimes painful, married life challenges our pride and squeezes out pet strongholds of selfishness. In essence, it teaches us sacrificial love, whether we like it or not. **Lesson number nine: Marriage is a greenhouse where God grows us into Christlikeness.**

Our honeymoon as a prophetic parable of our life together doesn't come close to covering the multitudinous lessons of marriage, but I hope it inspires readers who will marry to laugh and learn from our mistakes. Most importantly, I want to encourage ocean swimming couples to persistently embrace this beautiful, complicated, unpredictable alliance called marriage; a relationship God intends the world around us to behold as an illustration of the love of Christ (Ephesians 5:32).

QUESTIONS FOR REFLECTION AND DISCUSSION:

1. If you are married, what lessons would you add to the nine mentioned above?

2. From the reading above, answer this question: Why did God invent marriage? Add other reasons not mentioned in the reading.

3. If you are married, has God intervened at crucial times in your life together? Explain.

4. Why is marriage like a greenhouse?

5. How does marriage reflect Christ's love for the people of God?

6. What other thoughts or questions did the reading stir in you?

T(R)OPICAL READING BY SUBJECT

For convenience or felt needs below is an alternative reading plan. The readings can be loosely categorized into the following topics.

WORSHIP:

This category entails expressions of and encouragements to enhance the worship of God.

THE CHURCH:

These readings focus on the people of God with whom we swim and serve.

GOD STILL SPEAKS:

These readings invite us to listen for the various ways God communicates with us.

PRESSING IN:

These readings explore various classic Christian disciplines that make us better swimmers.

FINDING HEROES:

These readings are about finding models and mentors from whom we learn to be better swimmers.

EQUIPPING:

These readings aimed at preparing us to swim and serve well.

Headwinds:

Facing resistance and trouble are part of ocean swimming; these selections aim at strengthening us to continue with good courage.

Encouragements:

These readings are designed to breathe courage into us.

Challenges:

Swimming in the ocean is about challenge, risk taking and adventure. These selections focus on these challenges.

Calling:

Swimming includes personal mission. These selections invite us to find our own calling and act on it.

Friendly Advice:

These readings share my perspective on a few important issues you may face when ocean swimming.

About the Author

Barry pastored the Vineyard Christian church of Northern Kentucky for 29 years that grew to over a thousand members. He has served on the Vineyard national counsel and over the years participated in church planting efforts in the U.S., Guatemala, Mozambique, and Zimbabwe. After retiring from the pastorate in 2015, Barry is writing, continuing church planting work, and serving on the board of Reset Recovery ministries. Pastor Long resides in Northern Kentucky with his wife, France, three children, and eight grandchildren.

Made in the USA
Coppell, TX
11 November 2019